TO Thee I See

From picking in the fields of Texas to cooking for dignitaries on U.S. Navy ships, a journey I wouldn't change

★

Arby L. Hambric
with Trish Geran

Copyright © 2015 Arby L. Hambric
All rights reserved.
ISBN: 1505391687
ISBN-13: 978-1505391688

TO THEE I SEE: From picking in the fields of Texas to cooking for dignitaries on U.S. Navy ships, a journey I wouldn't change.

Narrated Arby L. Hambric
Written Trish Geran
Edited A.D. Hopkins & Trish Geran
Cover Design Arby L. Hambric & Trish Geran

All rights reserved. No part of this publication may be reproduced, stored in a retrieval system, or transmitted in any form or by any means-electronics, mechanical, photocopy, recording, or any other-except for brief quotations in printed reviews, without the prior permission of the publisher.

Hambric, Arby L.
Bibliography
- 1. Hambric, Arby L., 1926-
- 2. United States Navy 1945-1965
- 3. Blacks in the U.S. Navy
- 4. Blacks in the Military
- 5. Blacks who served in WWII
- 6. Blacks who served in Korean War
- 7. Blacks in Vietnam War
- 8. Blacks who served in the Military from 1945-1965

★ Dedication

For the Hambric family, may these precious memories and life changing lessons stored within these pages enrich your lives to the fullest as they have mine.

> 1) Coming together was a Begining and not an ending 2) Keeping together is Progress 3) working together is Success Jos. 1:5-9
> 4) i believe in the sun even when it not shining. 5) i believe in love, even when i am alone 6) i believe in god, even when he is silent 7) i believe if you Pay god Bill's he will Pay yours 8) like a wedding untill death do us Part: let us keep it that way.
>
> *Arly L. Hambrick*
>
> *Arthur L. Hambrick*
> *USN. Ret*

Acknowledgments

I could not have accomplished this goal without the assistance and encouragement of those who were supportive and trustworthy throughout this tiresome process. Ernest Busby, my brother-in-law since 1946, and whom I lost before the completion of this project, envisioned this long before I did. His admiration of my efforts in the military and in the community gave me courage to press on. My sister, Rosa Lee Haynes and cousin, Howard Hill researched additional information when I desperately needed it, and Hazel and Dedra Geran, and Eugene "Peve" Buford, who I miss terribly, took the time to read and edit multiple unfinished copies of the manuscript. Their prompt response and feedback gave me the confidence I needed to continue. Cecil Davis, my spiritual brother who helped me weather the storm, thank you for placing me on the right path. And my friend Judy McFadden who insisted I be open about my life suggested I approach author Trish Geran. In God's time, I met Ms. Geran and shared my most cherished, historical moments. I am grateful she did not allow the lack of details and my short memory about the past to hinder our progress.

Contents

DEDICATION
ACKNOWLEDGEMENTS

FOREWORD BY COLONEL GERALD D. CURRY

DARING GREATLY TO BELIEVE   12

In 1926, Arby is born on a dirt floor and shortly after his dad leaves. He works in the fields for six months and then attends school. After growing tired of trying to find work, a draft letter with a bus ticket arrives in the mail. The family collects $3.00 in change, the most he ever had to his name.

WHEN CALLED FOR DUTY   44

During the end of the WWII era in 1945, he is trained in a segregated Navy boot camp, passes the physical and fails the swimming demonstration but advances anyway. He becomes the Steward for the captain's staff, survives initiation, and on the way to Liberia meets men of distinction and dignitaries.

IN THE COMPANY OF MEN PLUS ONE   84

Jim Crow resurfaces and President Harry S. Truman arrives during freezing weather. Love blossoms but soon fades after his first son is born. The Korean War begins and life seems fragile on a Navy ship but he endures anyway. He remarries and is promoted on the admiral's staff.

WINDS OF CHANGE   130

Shortly after marrying Veronica in 1961, he learns her cousin is the first Black family to move into Compton and his brother-in-law admits he was more fascinated about playing baseball against Satchel Paige than becoming the first Black mayor of Teague, Texas.

PERIOD OF ADJUSTMENT   **143**

After learning that Veronica's cancer returned, he retires from the Navy to care for her. They relocate to his home in Teague, Texas but not even Momma Gussie's home-cooking could restore her health.

THEM BRIGHT LIGHTS   **163**

He relocates to Las Vegas and discovers the trappings of gambling. He finds a church home and directs a program and is immediately forced to deal with the kidnapping of one of its members. He returns home to say goodbye to his "real" father, but wasn't in time for his Momma Gussie. Appreciation for family suddenly becomes a priority.

THE WORTH OF IT ALL   **196**

He volunteers to be an escort at famed boxer Joe Louis' (Barrow) funeral and learns that Joe's wife Martha demanded that President Reagan bury him like a hero. After years of fighting the P.G.A., Joe Louis, Ted Rhodes, Billy Spiller, and John Shippen were finally granted a membership.

MIRACLE ON MADISON AVENUE   **211**

His church is given a name of distinction and the pastor and his wife become involved in illegal doings with a federal grant and is sentenced by the courts. For simply following the by-laws, Arby is removed from his post at the church.

CONTENT OF YOUR CHARACTER   **228**

For the first time, his health fails but he regains enough strength to receive the "War Hero" medal and to fight for the reopening of the only thoroughfare street in his community.

WHO IS DRIVING THIS MULE?   **260**
The right to vote and the importance of its history is expressed in a letter to First Lady Michelle Obama. A quick reference of the Buffalo Soldiers is made and feelings of being overlooked in the Navy are recalled, but the gratitude of being chosen to work among great men and to still be able to see far outweighs what once troubled his soul.

NOTES
  BIBLIOGRAPHY
INDEX

Foreword
COLONEL GERALD D. CURRY, USAF RET.

Arby L. Hambric takes us on a journey through a colorful past by giving us a glimpse of the segregated country in *To Thee I See: From picking in the fields of Texas to cooking for dignitaries on U.S. Navy ships, a journey I wouldn't change.*

His efforts uncover the depths of our existence by putting us center stage of several historical events that touched everyone's life at the time. Arby Hambric is an American veteran and hero in his own right who served in three war eras; World War II, the Korean War, and Vietnam War. Each of these episodes allowed him a front row view of history as it was unfolding. *To Thee I See* is a personal accounting of the disbanding of a segregated Armed Forces, and opening up of opportunities for people like you and I. Rarely, do we receive firsthand accounts and personal testimonies of side-bar conversations with iconic figures.

To Thee I See is a legacy project that will outlive its author, and serve as a roadmap of how he got over and through the harsh injustices of his time. It is an American story that reopens a painful racist past by illustrating how a triumphant people with a strong belief in God were forced to overcome adversity at every measure. I am impressed with Mr. Hambric's strength of character and willingness to open up to the world by sharing his life. He does so with conviction and passion by leaving a path of genuine authenticity rarely experienced.

Mr. Hambric's wisdom offers timeless advice in the sense that this project is honest and has a sincere tone. When faced against severe odds in his early years in Teague, Texas, Arby Hambric learned to understand the realities of racism and surviving a Jim Crow South. These tough lessons armed him with the necessary tools to successfully navigate and out maneuver racism he would face while serving in the Navy. During this period he was often the only African American assigned to his unit. Racism rarely distracted him, or held him back. Mr. Hambric continued to keep himself grounded with a strong believe in his abilities and the spiritual foundation he obtained as a child.

To Thee I See is a must read for anyone who wants to walk through a historical time capsule and see what every day African Americans did to get along. His story is a simple, yet a complex one because of the impact he made on society and most importantly his family. Arby Hambric has a story to tell, and you should listen to his wise counsel. He touches on the highs and lows of life, and explains that while in your everyday doings, you have tremendous opportunities to inspire greatness in others. Mr. Hambric's writings helps his readers understand that the small things we accomplish everyday has a way of lasting a lifetime and can potentially touch millions. This is a story about strength of family, love, sincere gratitude to a nation who did not recognize the dedicated service of one of its own. It is a story of conviction, dedication, and seeing-it-through. After reading *To Thee I See*, you will feel like a favorite son or daughter of Arby Hambric, because of his captivating stories. I am completely honored and humbled to have the opportunity to support this endeavor. Arby Hambric is our American hero!

My responsibility, our responsibility as lucky Americans, is to try to give back to this country as much as it has given us, as we continue our American journey together.

General Colin Powell
Diplomat - Military Leader

One

DARING GREATLY TO BELIEVE

I, Arby Lee Hambric, was born on November 24, 1926, in Centerville, Texas, on the dirt floor of a one-room, tin shack we were ashamed to proudly call home. The day Momma began to feel me moving something terrible inside, Grandma Loraine was already in route by way of horse and buggy from Marquez, Texas, which was about 21 miles away. She walked in the door wearing her midwife hat-rolling up her sleeves, boiling pots of hot water, and gathering clean towels. It only took a few minutes to spit me out. Momma was 19 years old and said she had things to do and wasting time on something as trivial as labor pains was not one of them.

My dearest Grandma Loraine was determined that her first grandson by her youngest daughter would come into the world kicking and screaming. She recorded the time of my birth as 9:13 p.m. on a cloth napkin and placed it in the middle of an old worn family Bible. Then she gave me my name and prophesized it would make me famous one day.

At that time, the population was 320, and 40 percent of that number were Black folks. It was a period of hardship and we were in search of an identity. The town's Whites did not care to know our names; they were only interested in who would work the most for less pay. Although our sense of reality was a constant uphill battle, we learned to fix our minds just to make it from one day to the next simply because we were Black and for no other reason.

When I was a little boy, my momma told me that a Black man who was falsely accused of killing a White man was dragged from his jail cell and hung on an oak tree called, "Tree of Justice." White folks gathered like spectators at a boxing match. It became a game of sport to lynch a Black man every Friday night except for this preacher. They waited after he delivered his Sunday sermon to hang him. Centerville was no longer just a small town that existed in the shadows of Dallas and Houston, it was now the offspring of the "White Man's Black."

Every July, the town would celebrate Independence Day by hosting a Black-Eye Pea Festival filled with an array of activities and an allotment of fireworks. But we Blacks didn't care much about these traditions. One served as a reminder of how we continued to be enslaved *after* the Declaration of Independence was signed, and the latter, well who do you think picked those peas? I agree with Frederick Douglas who said, "What to the slave is the Fourth of July?"

My momma and daddy, Gussie McAdams and Sam Hambric, Jr., were born in Waxahachie, Texas, in July of 1907. Momma knew her birthday was on the seventh of that month but daddy didn't have a clue. They didn't talk much about their childhood. A few times they blurted a few disturbing incidents that only confirmed their belief that the world was without sympathy, but nothing in its entirety. Momma's parents, Grandma Lorraine and Grandpa John, reacted in the same manner.

I was five years old when I first met my Uncle Joe Hambric. I had one pair of shoes I could only wear to church and school. In the background was our outhouse.

Cousin Henry McAdam's tin shack looked identical to the one I was born in.

Grandma was knowledgeable about the history of the task masters and slavery, and could tell Jim Crow a thing or two. Momma said she had a lot of horrid experiences when she was a kid, "the worst anyone could go through in a lifetime" but she never told me what that was and nor did I ever come close to discovering what she meant. In other words, a conversation about days of growing up in the bowels of Texas during segregation was highly unlikely.

My dad Sam left shortly after I learned to walk and when my sister, Rosa Lee was still in my mother's "oven." I could not for the life of me remember what he looked like. It's not like anyone in the neighborhood owned a camera. I didn't recall anything special about his character and I wasn't told why he never came back. In those days, it wasn't customary for a kid to question grown folk's business. One time my cousin asked his momma if her boyfriend was the father of a kid in his class who had the same last name and she knocked him into middle of next week looking both ways for Sunday.

Over the next eight years, Sam would make an occasional "I was in the neighborhood" visit. After spending quality moments with his nearby relatives and god knows who else, he thought enough of us to stop by to say hello. My image of him became nothing more than a revolving door.

Momma didn't believe in letting grass grow under her feet and those pit stops Sam made didn't amount to much. She felt that if she couldn't be the cake, damn the crumbs. She met and married a man named Artice Lankford and shortly after, my youngest sister Mildred was born. There were more mouths to feed so it was getting harder to make ends meet. Living in "the country", we didn't have many options. We either worked in the fields picking vegetables and fruits and cutting sugar cane, or Momma would do domestic work for a "good" White family. She started working when she was around nine years old. The grown folks believed when you knew right from wrong you were old enough to work.

Artice suggested we relocate to Teague, which was 33 minutes from Centerville. He said times would be better and we would have a chance of making a decent living. Momma believed in taking risks. She said that no one was going to drop anything in her lap but a washtub full of soiled laundry that needed to be washed and ironed. We packed a few sacks of personal belongings and caught the bus to Teague. The heaviest "bag" I carried was full of hope and promise.

During this period, the country had just survived the Great Depression and was enjoying the repeal of Prohibition. We lived off what was handed to us, Black history was in question, and Jim Crow was alive and active. We left the old landmark and down through the years we struggled and worked for very little pay. Our Black preachers were not corrupt; they were honest. After working in the fields all day, sometimes instead of getting paid they were given eggs and milk, which would spoil by the time they made it home. It was common for Blacks to be owed more money than what they made. Families and neighbors learned how to stay together and raise their own food. There was no provision out there or any way out, and God help all of us if just one was caught stealing or embezzling from the White man. The whole race would take the blame for the illicit actions of one.

When we arrived in Teague, I thought we were still in Centerville. Artice moved us into a shack that was built with galvanized tin and burlap, similar to the one back home. The ceiling had a gap so wide I could see the stars at night. During heavy downpours of rain, we would place large tin tubs under it and then use the fresh water to drink and clean clothes. The landlord was not responsible for repairs, and Artice, bless his heart, was no handyman so we learned to live with our shortcomings. I was 12 years old and was willing to help out in any way I could but Artice didn't have any skills to teach me besides yard work and I already had those before he joined the family. Momma told us to be loyal to his promise of better days ahead and that everyone deserved a second chance.

In time, contrary to what Artice believed, Momma concluded that the industry in Teague would not and could not provide better days and the options for survival were too darn similar to the ones in Centerville. She grew leery of his vision and doubted his ability as a provider. I remember overhearing her tell Grandma that most of the time he was so broke he couldn't jump over a nickel to save a dime. One day, he told us kids to tell "your momma" he was going to the store and would be back, but he never returned. It took longer to get over Artice than my dad Sam, and when I did, I learned how to lower my expectations; it was the only way I knew how to keep the pain from reoccurring.

Momma started working for a White family where the bread winner was a mail carrier. We referred to them as "The Smiths." They were so comfortable with her and us kids coming and going from their home they insisted we live in the servant quarters, which was located in the back. Momma gladly welcomed that offer. They paid her $3.00 a week to do domestic chores such as cleaning, ironing, cooking, and whatever else was needed to continue the daily flow. We were like family so when it was harvest time for cotton, which was July to mid-December, The Smiths would find a temporary replacement so Momma could travel to Midland, Texas, to work in the fields. Picking cotton earned more than domestic work, but only if "Mr. Charlie" paid an honest wage for an honest day of work.

Instead of going to school, Momma thought it would be best for us to work in the fields. She received very little education because she had to drop out and begin working at a young age. She was taught the three R's: reading, writing, and arithmetic, but was never satisfied with what she knew and vowed to do something about it one day. At least were getting some schooling instead of none-she was proud about that.

Harvest time was like a mini-family reunion; it

was the one time besides a funeral I saw my relatives. We would pile in old pick-up trucks until we were packed like sardines and caravan with the scorching sun roasting on the sides of our neck and the hot breeze blowing in every direction. We could only pray to make it without one of the trucks breaking down but that was rare. One time, the rear axle broke. We just curled up in the truck's nine foot bed made from wood and slept until the next morning. After a few of the men pieced a few scraps of metal together to repair the wheel we continued our journey until we reached our destination, which lasted approximately seven long and sweaty hours.

    We would start picking cotton just before sunrise and way past sundown. The length of the sack was eight feet long and the average weight we turned in at the end of the day was no less than 70 pounds, which was more than what I weighed soaking wet. A few weeks later, Momma had us revisit the rows we picked to get what she called "the late bloomers." The money we made from that batch afforded us to buy a Christmas gift for the family, which was normally a pair of socks or a scarf. I was sure the money we earned picking in the fields all day was put in the slop jar for "rainy days" but I later found out it was simply to make both ends meet instead of just one.

When harvest was over and the New Year had begun, we attended Booker T. Washington, an all-Black high school in Teague, grades 1 through 12. On the first day, the teachers would have our assignments prepared to take home. I fought like heck to make up for missed days even though they didn't hold you back if you failed to complete most of them. I had a hard time completing a few of my lessons, which caused me to always find myself a few steps behind.

Our books were handed down from the White schools. There would be so many pages torn, missing, or marked excessively with crayons it was virtually impossible to piece together the overall lesson. There were even times we didn't have access to a different book until a few semesters later. We made good of the ones in the classroom no matter how moth-eaten they were or how many times we had read them. I enjoyed learning, but I swear there were days we were so broke the hunger pains made it hard for me to focus on what the teacher was saying.

My sisters and I walked to school every bit of a mile each way. For lunch, Momma would pack homemade biscuits with molasses in the middle in a tin lunch pail, which looked like a mop bucket except it was approximately three times smaller and came with a fitting lid. Every once in a while she would surprise us by placing an apple or an orange.

School was one of the two places I could wear my black leather shoes. The other time was to church. The second I hit the front door, I had to place them back into the original shoe box. For the remainder of the day, we went barefoot. In the summer, we learned to walk at a much faster pace so the dirt roads wouldn't blister our feet. When we worked in the fields, we wore the handed-down shoes that were given to Momma from the White families.

Momma ordered our shoes from the "Sears, Roebuck and Company" catalog. We tried them on the second they arrived because Sears had a "no return" policy. If they were a little snug, we would hold on to the bed post until our foot was all the way inside. If that didn't work, we would cut a small incision on the sides where the big and little toe was located. All we could do was pray that the leather would stretch after wearing it for a short duration of time.

The catalog was our access to new clothing and shoes because the closest retail store was in Waco, Texas, which was at that time 60 miles away. And because transportation was a necessity not a luxury, we could only afford to catch the bus a few times a year.

On Saturday mornings, it was customary to walk about three hours into town to buy food. Every once in a while we got lucky and caught a wagon ride with a family member who lived in our neighborhood.

Momma would take advantage of this opportunity and buy items for people she knew were in need. It was also a way of eliminating them from borrowing a commodity "every time she looked up."

Momma would buy large bags of rice, beans, flour, sugar, yellow corn meal, several cans of lard, and a few glassed jars of molasses. Even though she knew how to squeeze a buffalo off a nickel and hold a quarter so tight the eagle screamed, she was well aware that the White store clerk practiced what we called the "thumb-scale measurement"; it was when the cashier would place their thumb on the scale to increase the weight. In other words, if she paid for 48 pounds, she was only going home with 42 of it. They took advantage of the fact we lacked education and had little or no transportation to travel to the nearest store, which was more than likely located several miles away.

Momma would empty the commodities into containers, clean the croaker sacks they came in on a rub-board and make clothes with the cloth. On a small wood burning stove, she would prepare food for an entire week. We didn't have a refrigerator, but when we were blessed with meat of any kind it was packed with salt and then placed in a smokehouse, which was located in the backyard.

On Sunday mornings, we attended the United Methodist Church. If Momma went, we went and no one questioned her. The church was once an old house. A large wooden cross hung by the pulpit and a framed picture of the universal depiction of what Jesus looked decorated the middle of the back wall.

Momma was an active, long-time member and when she walked in those double doors, the usher politely escorted her to "her" seat. We often attended Sunday school that is if the teacher or a replacement showed up. After class, we would sit by Momma like little puppies. We knew to be quiet and still otherwise she would give us a stare that promised a whippin' when we got home.

Service started at ten o'clock in the morning until

three in the afternoon. Sometimes it lasted until late in the evening. During the summer, there was one fan that was supposed to cool the room down but instead it did nothing but circulate the hot air. When we got home our clothes would be wringing wet.

The neighborhood was so quiet the nearby residents could hear the tambourine playing and the choir singing. At the end of the sermon, our preacher would yell at the top of his lungs. They called that a hermetic sermon also referred to as "whopping." It supposed to be like an opera, but most of the time the piercing, high pitched tone did nothing more than cause my ears to ring.

I wanted to learn how to be an effective Christian so I enrolled in Vacation Bible School at our church. The more training I received and the more knowledge I gained I still found myself recalling what my Uncle Henry, a Baptist preacher, once told me when I was 10 years old. He said, "Son, a White man government the White man's religion is not worth a damn. Where ever you go, whatever you do always remember to stay close to God." Those words played in my head like a broken record. I heard what he said but I didn't understand what he meant or maybe I didn't want to because it interrupted my mission of becoming the type of man I thought Christ wanted me to be.

After years of putting away a few pennies, we were finally able to move into a house built from quality wood with an extra room. It was definitely an upgrade, but the one downfall was that the hallway was so small two people passing by would rub shoulders. The rent was $1.50 a month, and there was always a relative or time so there was no relative or distant cousin living with us for a short length of time so there was no such thing as having a room or a bed with your name on it. During the winter, it would get so cold my we would jump into our bed to keep each other warm.

Momma worked for a banker named Mr. Curry and his son Pete and I became close friends. We played every day after school until supper was ready. Momma

Left: Aunt Mary Cole, Uncle O.C. Hall, Momma Gussie, and Cousin Minnie Watts after service at United Methodist Church in Teague, Texas. Uncle O.C. would later relocate to Las Vegas.

would serve his family and I would go home to warm up the left-over food that was either in the icebox, if we could afford to buy ice that week, or in a paper bag near the creek that ran along the back of our house. The cool breeze from the water was an alternative way to keep food items fresh that would spoil when left at room temperature. At first I thought I was told to leave because of that old saying "a white man eat and run, a Nigga sit and make room for more." But it was because there was no place for a colored person at a White person's table. It just wasn't normal.

I was permitted to walk to someone's house only if it was a few feet away. But when that sun went down I'd better high-tail it home because if an aunt, uncle, cousin, or neighbor caught me they would light fire under my biscuits. My sisters and I were only disciplined a few times and that was from being disobedient while Momma was at work. She would make us go to bed, and when the clock struck twelve o'clock, we would undress and stand still and take that whippin' like a champ.

The first hate sign I saw in Teague, Texas, read, "No Niggers Allowed After Sundown." It was "understood", according to Jim Crow, that Blacks who worked for Whites had to return to their neck of the woods when it was dark outside.

Jim Crow was the most degrading depiction of Blacks in the history of this country. He was a character created in 1828, by a man named, Thomas Dartmouth "Daddy" Rice. Dressed in ragged clothes and blackface makeup, he performed his minstrel act in front of an all-White audience. With his hands on his hips, he would strut across the stage and jokingly portray Blacks as buffoons who loved ole' massa but hated themselves. He painted a convincing picture of a content Negro singing and working in the cotton fields all day, gobbling chittlins' and slurping on watermelons that more than likely were stolen. Surely one would think that the singing and dancing at the end of the day was an indication of how grateful they were to live on a plantation and to have an owner who loved him some "niggras." But that was hardly the case.

Rice wanted the world to believe that Blacks were full of fear and incapable of thinking for themselves and therefore can't and won't leave the plantation even if you handed them their freedom papers on a silver platter. Grandma Loraine said that the most valuable slave wasn't the hardest worker or the one who picked the most cotton he was the one who could entertain the best.

One night, the David family hosted a party and asked my cousin Tela to work late. They promised to make sure she got home safe, but when the party was over and she asked Mr. David to accompany her home he said, "Nigga' I'm too drunk and too tired to go anywhere." Tela proceeded down the dark dirt roads praying the whole time for protection. A White man sitting on his front porch drinking a beer noticed her when she walked by. He picked up his shotgun and yelled, "There is a darkie around here!"

I grew up believing that White people treated their dogs better than us but I refused to allow this notion to interfere with my decision of whether or not to be friends with someone because of the color of their skin. I had family members who refused to think that way, but that was their problem, not mine.

My other White friend was named Charlie Levels. We would walk along the side of highway "Route 74" and make-believe we were on our way somewhere of the utmost importance. One day, we saw a former schoolmate walking on the other side of the road. He was wearing an Army uniform and I near-bout lost it. I marveled at this Black officer the way I did at the impeccable exterior paint on the Curry's house. It started me thinking about what life would be like in the military. I wasn't close to anyone who was active in the service, and I only had a short conversation with a few of them when they came home on leave, which was either for a funeral or a family emergency. The lack of first-hand knowledge didn't hinder my vision of one day wearing one of those brown jackets. I wasn't afraid of engaging in battle; what scared me to death was that my life would end up amounting to nothing worth mentioning.

I spent the majority of my summers with Grandma Loraine and Grandpa John in Marquet, Texas. Being in their presence was always uplifting. There was no such thing as a summer job; it was called chores and Grandma Loraine always had them waiting for me the second I step in the door. She would use her fingers to count the things that needed to be done around the house or in the yard. Even if my visit was for only one day, she found things for me to do. She used to tell me, "An idle mind is the devil's workshop."

They grew 100 pound watermelons on vines that extended seven feet long. I would eat the heart of the melon until my stomach poked out, and then I would throw the scraps to the hogs or back into the watermelon patch for the birds. While Grandpa pulled the ears of corn from the stalks in the fields, Grandma

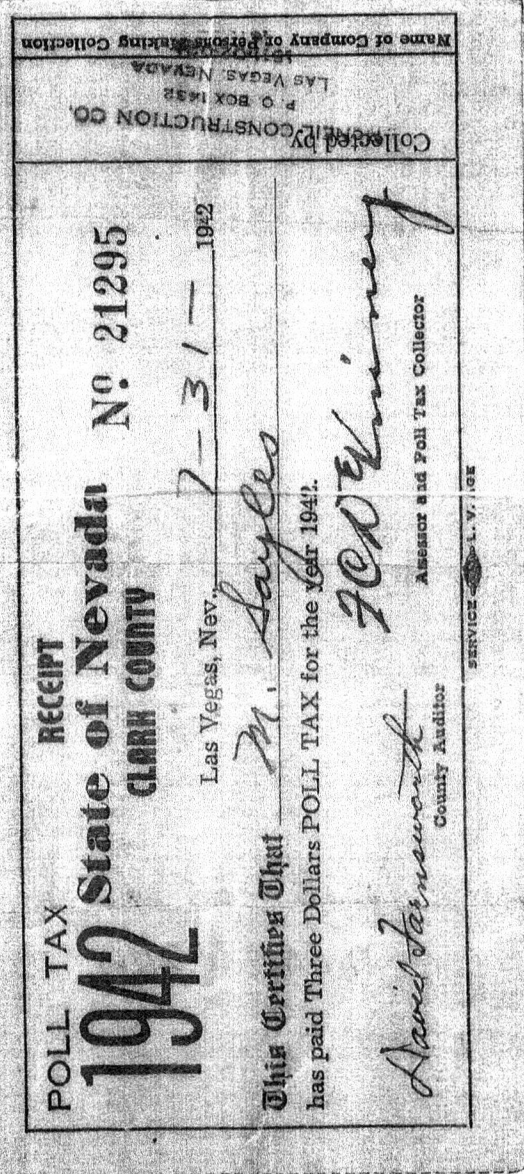

POLL TAX **1942** RECEIPT
State of Nevada
CLARK COUNTY

No. 21295

Las Vegas, Nev., 7-31- 1942

This Certifies That M. Sayles
has paid Three Dollars POLL TAX for the Year 1942.

David Farnsworth
County Auditor

JCO'Whinney
Assessor and Poll Tax Collector

SERVICE — L.V. JCE

Collected by
BOULDER CONSTRUCTION CO.
P. O. BOX 1452
LAS VEGAS, NEVADA
Name of Company or Persons Making Collection

showed me how to make buttermilk. I would pour the milk in a three gallon butter churn crock, move the plunger up and down until the liquid was clabbered, and wait until the cream separated and the butter rose to the top. We baked cornbread with it and sometimes we drank it for breakfast, lunch, and dinner because it was all we had. She taught me how to pick peas and feed the hogs. When the kids in school found out, they started calling me "Poor Pig." They also thought the name fit me perfect because I was skinny and lousy in sports.

Every once in a while I found work cutting grass with my push lawnmower. I charged ¢.25 a yard no matter how large it was and that included the sides and back. I will never forget when I went back home with $1.25 in my pocket. I was so proud of myself, I bragged to my sisters and friends in the neighborhood. When Momma found out, she deflated my chest and asked for every cent. She said she needed it to buy food for the family. I didn't resist because that was something I was always willing to contribute towards. All I wanted was enough to buy an ice cream cone, but she said it wasn't about what I wanted it was about what we needed.

The radio was our only connection to the outside world. I listened to shows like *Red Skelton, Redd Foxx, Amos 'n' Andie*, and championship boxing matches. When the heavyweight boxing champ, Joe Louis fought every radio in the United States tuned in to listen.

I will never forget his first match against the German, Max Schmeling. It was on June 22, 1936, and Max threw a punch that knocked Joe out cold in the 12th round. The second time they fought was on June 22, 1938. Two minutes and four seconds in the first round, Joe threw a punch that knocked Schmeling flat on his back. The referee counted to 10 and when he announced Joe Louis as the heavyweight champion of the world we cheered at the top of our lungs. White Americans felt like they had just defeated Germany, and Black folks felt they had emerged from slavemanship to championship thanks to their "Great

Black Hope."

Momma Gussie believed the third time was a charm because two wasn't enough and four was too many. That was definitely true about Charlie Levels, her last and third husband. He was the dad we always longed for. He had the same name as my White friend so I figured that must be a sign from up above.

Charlie was a hard-working man with good intentions. Momma said he promised to take care of her and us kids and she trusted his every word. She knew in order to earn a living in Teague meant you had to use every imaginative bone in your body. Charlie would clean flower beds, mow grass, pick peas, and cotton. He was slow with his speech, but quick to open his heart. He was personable and he taught me to look people in the eye when conversing with them because it showed respect and proved you were listening.

On the days I worked with Charlie in the scorching hot sun, the humidity left me feeling like a prune. I was so exhausted at the end of the day I was tempted to fall asleep on anybody's clothes line, but somehow I always managed to make it home.

One time, when school was in recess and before the cotton was ready to be harvested, I stayed with family members in Fortworth, Texas, I worked as a porter at a nearby café. I was 16 years old and it was my first "real" job. I interviewed and started that very same day. I didn't even have to fill out an application or submit any documents. I felt good about being away from home especially from Momma, which was a surprise to me.

During my break, I read in the local newspaper that Armour & Company's packing house was in need of a meat packer. I was hired on the spot and when they told me I would be making $25 a week I fell against the wall. It was the most anybody in my family had ever earned. Even though my salary allowed me the opportunity to send money back home, the living conditions in Fort Worth were worse than those in Teague and Centerville put together. I was paying a price no matter which road I took so I went back home.

On November 24, 1944, when I turned 18 years old, I received a letter to register with the United States military draft board. The words clearly stated that it was my legal obligation as a United States citizen, and if I refused charges of "draft dodging" would be brought against me followed by time in prison. I filled out the form and signed my name on the dotted line. When I mailed in the "U.S. Postage Paid" envelope, I didn't think much about the military. The only thing on my mind was graduating from Booker T. Washington High School. It was starting to bother me that I was 18 years old and I was a few years short from completing my diploma.

I will never forget the first week of August in 1945. One afternoon, I walked in the door carrying a pile of homework when Momma handed me a letter addressed from the United States Military. I dropped the books and ripped open the envelope. As I unfolded the perfectly typed letter, I discovered a bus ticket. The words were few and to the point; I had been drafted and was to report immediately to the induction center in Dallas, Texas.

It felt good reading that letter, but Momma was neutral and Charlie understood because he served in World War I, but refused to talk about his experience. She knew it wasn't an option and there was a chance I wouldn't make it back home. This new beginning came at a time when I was at my wits end and fed up with pushing against that stubborn racial wall in Texas. I was starting to feel like a burden to my family incapable of providing assistance to help with the daily necessities in our home, and going back to Fort Worth was not even a thought. In Centerville and Teague, every opportunity for Black folks came with a sacrifice of self, and any glimmer of hope was soon washed away by senseless acts of discrimination. The military would not serve as an inconvenience or obligation it would be a way out.

After Momma calmed down and made peace

with the idea of her only son leaving to as she called it "no man's land", my family scrapped together pennies, nickels, dimes, and quarters. On the day I was scheduled to leave, I kissed my family and walked out the door wearing my broken-in leather shoes. In one hand was a burlap sack of toiletries and in the other was a one-way ticket. I smiled and felt proud when I tugged on my pocket because pinned inside was a folded white starched handkerchief with $3.00 in change. It was the most money I ever had to my name.

- - - It is Written - - -

Two

WHEN CALLED
FOR DUTY

I caught the Greyhound bus to Dallas, Texas. When I arrived at the induction center, the line for registration was so long it wrapped around the building. Four hours later, I was finally able to sit at a desk to be processed. I answered questions, signed documents, was finger printed and then given a complete physical, dental, and eye exam. It was similar to being booked into jail except the one phone call would come later. Because the military was aware that 85% of the Black men drafted could not read or write and for those of us who could, it was not beyond a ninth grade level, they were instructed to enlist them no matter how damning the results. On August 16th, I passed all of the exams and was told my branch of service would be the United States Navy. The next step was to catch a chartered bus to the United States Naval Training Center Bainbridge in Bainbridge, Maryland.

On the ride over, one of the men said a scuttlebutt was that the Navy was the most segregated of all branches but it was recently announced that the training camp would be integrated. When I arrived, there were 20,000 Black men training in platoons of 20-30 led mostly by White drill instructors.

Although World War II ended in Europe on May 7, 1945, and President Truman ordered atomic bombs to be dropped on the Japanese cities, Hiroshima on August 6, and Nagasaki on August 9, which resulted in Japan's Emperor Hirohito announcing in a recorded radio address the surrender of Japan to the Allies on August 14, the military continued to enforce the draft after WWII was supposedly over. We had governmental authority to occupy and rehabilitate the countries we defeated so more men would be needed to maintain this "Occupation." I had no idea what was expected of me in the Navy. I was young, had my hair combed to the front and was full of myself, but if you stood close enough you could hear my knees just a knockin'.

We were assigned a tour guide to make sure our in-processing went smooth. Because we were considered illiterate, all of our instructions were given orally. Not one document was handed out in case we forgot some of the important points that were emphasized. We ate like pigs in the Mess Hall and when we were done we cleaned our areas and stood. All of a sudden, our guide's voice changed from nice and soft to mean and loud. That's when I knew I was in the Navy.

Inside a large room were rows of long wooden tables with clothing attire that came in only white and blue. I emptied my personal belongings out the burlap sack and undressed behind a screen. I then placed my civilian clothes inside a box which was scheduled to be mailed the following day back home to Momma.

Also on the table was a G.I. (general issue), which included a sea bag, dog tags, miscellaneous clothing, hygiene products, and survival items such as salt tablets, and long-johns also referred to as skivvies, which were worn under the uniform for unbearable winter days.

I called Momma to let her know I was enlisted and all was "hunky dory." I wanted to tell her that Jim Crow was at the campsite and he brought his cousins, but I didn't want to ruffle her feathers. Momma used to say, don't worry about the mule, just load the wagon. I thought it would be wise to adhere to her advice.

A buzz cut was next on the agenda. I flopped in the barber chair and before I could scoot down a little, lumps of hair started tumbling off my shoulders and in my lap. I felt rebellious and thought about the big afros the "Negro Calvary", famously known as the Buffalo Soldiers, sported when they fought in the after the Civil War. The Indians gave them that name because their hair reminded them of the shaggy, long coat on a buffalo. When I stood up, I was bald as an eagle. I looked in the mirror closer and couldn't believe the odd shape of my head. But I refused to let it get me down because for the first time in my life I was where I thought I was supposed to be.

During condition training, a drill instructor

taught us physical drills such as push-ups and duck-walking. With our shoulders back and chin up, we marched in place and then up and down a hill for several miles. I learned the position of attention, to talk only when spoken to, and how to fire and execute a weapon and gracefully hold it when standing at attention and at parade rest.

We were required to swim even though the military was fully aware public pools were off limit to most Black Southerners. We were given a few lessons and a few days later a demonstration was expected. It was sink or swim and most of us sank, but they advanced us anyway.

The only allowance we received was $10, and two weeks later $5. We called these earnings the "Flying 10" because it was spent before you could count it; and "Leaping 5", it jumped out your hand the second you touched it. The purpose of the money was to purchase toiletries at the P.X. (Post Exchange) store. After eight weeks, and that includes P-Week, I completed basic training and was no closer to knowing how to swim than the first day I arrived. I was classified a Steward and was assigned on the escort carrier USS *Palau* CVE-122. But before I would receive training for that position, it was mandatory to take a week off to visit my family before heading out to sea.

I wanted to be in high cotton when I stepped on that bus. I got all gussied up in white from head to toe and wore that Navy uniform like it was designed just for me. With my head in the air, I looked the bus driver in the eye and spoke and then proudly sat in the front seat. He yelled, "Boy get yo' Black ass in the back and know yo' place!" My feelings were hurt. As I slowly gathered my courage off the floor, it was obvious that because of the color of my skin the uniform didn't mean a darn thing.

My family greeted me with open arms. Momma and Charlie added a bedroom and front porch onto the house that was surrounded by green grass and a vegetable garden. The folks from my old neighborhood came over with dishes of soul food and asked a lot of questions. I stretched the truth and bent the facts. I told colorful stories and overlooked the ones in shades of grey. It bothered me to lie because Momma said a conversation could change a person's life, but I continued to stick with my version of the truth. I wasn't ready for them to know that I was risking my life for a military that treated us like second-class citizens.

When I returned, the Black sailors were allowed to ride in the Pullman quarters on the train from Bainbridge to the Naval Reserve Training Center in Tacoma, Washington. I was taught how to make beds, cook and serve three squares, and pick up. As a Steward, my job was to assist the needs of the officers and maintain their state room, which was also called their living quarters. I mopped and cleaned the "heads" in assigned areas or whatever a White sailor, even if he was of a lower rank, asked me to do.

The Whites were ranked Seamen; they were never classified a Steward. Their duties were engineering,

In 1946, days before the USS *Palau* was scheduled to launch, Captain W.E. Cleaves (seated at the head of the table) and Lieutenant Commander W.C. Fitzpatrick (right-front) hosted a dinner at the Naval Reserve Training Center in Tacoma, Washington. I was in training at the time and my duty was to take the officer's top coats and hats.

plastering walls, painting, and welding. In other words, the Blacks did what the Whites did not have to do. The ship was separated by rank and segregated by race and because there were at least 20 divisions of men, racial discrimination was much more apparent than it was at boot camp.

I recalled the time a former schoolmate, Willie Moore, who had joined the Navy in 1942, came home for a few days during a two week leave. I went by to see him, to touch his medals, but there wasn't anything to rub but his bald head. He looked the same except for a touch of sadness in his eyes. I was fascinated with the military, at least the uniforms, and he knew it. He felt compelled, however, to tell me that a scuttlebutt was that the Secretary of the Navy, Frank Knox, publically stated that "no Filipino, no Black man would get no further in his man Navy than the kitchen." That was then and I thought for sure by this time the perception of Black enlisted men would have changed but it had not. I swallowed my pride and accepted my position. I stopped dreaming of medals and stripes and how important I would feel wearing these distinguished honors and decided to concentrate on making it back home in one piece.

The USS *Palau* CVE-122 was commissioned for sea duty on January 15, 1946. After passing the shakedown cruise, she sailed from the Pudget Sound Naval Base, located 33 miles from Tacoma, through the Panama Canal and the Atlantic Ocean to her destination, the Norfolk Naval Base in Norfolk, Virginia. When my sea sickness finally calmed down, I settled into the "colored" Steward's quarters. The berthing area consisted of beds with a thin mattress placed on top of a rack that was stacked three deep, and the shower and "head" were located next to it. Our clothing items were stenciled with our last name and first name initial, which made it easier for the laundry person on duty to sort. The storage locker was so small I had to roll my clothes like a newspaper and place my hat on top of my shoes.

At 1600, it was time for liberty and a group of us newly enlisted men grew curious about our surroundings. We caught the streetcar to Norfolk and on the way we played a card game called "Street-Car Molly." The dealer would shuffle a deck of cards and distribute three cards faced down until someone named the "money card." When we reached our destination, the only one who wasn't broke was the dealer. It was the classic short-con game with the cards more than likely marked and the edges bent.

After walking down a few streets, I grew tired of hanging around my shipmates so I took off in another direction. While embracing the cool breeze from the Elizabeth River and Chesapeake Bay, I toured the historic sites and marveled at the bronze statues of legendary figures. I was amazed to discover that a Black man named, Joseph Jenkins Roberts, who was born in Norfolk became the first and seventh President of Liberia.

I walked further into town and ended up on

Hampton Boulevard, a congested area with locals and tourists. Up and down the road were wall-to-wall beer joints, brothels, motels, gambling joints, just about every type of an establishment that could separate a sailor from his money.

Since none of my shipmates were in sight, I headed back to catch the next streetcar and there they were, beautifully displayed on a plush green lawn, were two signs that read, "Dogs and Sailors Keep Off The Grass" and "Rather Have A Dog Than A Black Sailor." I wasn't moved by these words because Momma had written me a letter warning me about some of Virginia's history. Her employer was a history buff and she took advantage of reading his books when she was home alone.

She said a man named Willie Lynch gave a speech in 1712, on the James River, which was a short distance from where I was docked. He was a slave owner and swore that the best way to enslave the minds of the Negro for 300 years was to pit the young against the old, light-skinned against the dark-skinned, the female against the male, and the house Negro against the field Negro. In other words, he believed there was more than one way to keep the Negro in chains.

Even though I had more time on my 42 hour liberty pass, I got off the streetcar a few blocks from the entrance of the Naval Base. As I walked towards the ship, I stopped and looked at the magnitude of its dimensions and then glanced at the lower deck. Not only did the *Palau* complement 1,066 crew members, she 34 fighter planes parked on the hanger deck with the wings folded upward, an invention supposedly created by a Black man named Herman L. Grimes, but according to the military a similar invention was already recorded two years prior to the date he officially filed, which was on September 22, 1938.

Grime's invention allowed the pilot from the cockpit to pivot the aircraft wings to a vertical folded upward position on a multi-engine plane after landing. This maneuver enabled the Navy ships to gain more aircraft superiority, which was the advantage the Japanese Navy had when they bombed Pearl Harbor on the morning of 07 December 1941. Despite years of fighting for recognition, he was told the idea came from someone else's patent.

Herman L. Grimes was a country boy from Alabama and a recipient of the Purple Heart Medal in WWII. His son, Herman L. Grimes, Jr., said that when his father died in 1970, he went to his grave with a broken heart.

When I returned on the ship, I told a few guys about my unusual visit to Norfolk. They hit the deck laughing at how wet I was behind the ears. In between the chuckles, I was told that the city's reputation was so bad that sailors named it "Shit City" and the best way to see ole nasty Norfolk was through a rear view mirror.

After four months of being docked at home port, I was comfortable carrying out my duties as a Steward for the commissioned officers. Then to my surprise, I was reassigned to be the Steward for Captain Cleaves. I went from peeling potatoes for 60-70 commissioned officers in the Wardroom to assisting one person and his guests, which was never expected to be more than 20 people. I was the only Black from the Steward Division, which consisted of Blacks and Filipinos, chosen for this assignment.

Some of the Black sailors thought they were better qualified than me while others wanted to be my friend because they knew I would be given a lot of favors. For example, if my uniform wasn't spotless and pressed I could send it back to the laundry or tailor department. I had access to the captain's car to run errands when we were in port, could request additional time on my liberty, and ate whatever I desired regardless if it was on the menu for the day. I was so defined in my position I earned the nickname "Captain." For the first time in my life, I felt relaxed around people from the White race. It was a privilege and honor to be selected to work on the captain's staff but man was I nervous.

Captain Willis E. Cleaves (left) and Lieutenant Commander W.C. Fitzpatrick were the first leaders on the USS *Palau* escort carrier.

The USS *Palau* was commissioned for sea duty on January 15, 1946. Today, I am one of the oldest living plank owners.

A Filipino guy named, Laboa was the Chief Steward over the Captain's Mess, which meant he was in charge of the pantry (kitchen) and the upkeep of the dining room. He and I would get together and plan the Captain's menu two-weeks in advance. We would place a food order for upcoming special events discuss the arrangements and designs, the colors of the candles, and the type of flowers for the center pieces. Our intention was to store enough food in the freezers below deck that would last at least 3 months. While at sea, if we were running short, a cargo ship would make a special trip to fill the order.

I prepared three meals a day for Captain Cleaves, took care of his clothing and sleeping quarters-state room-and made sure a fresh pot of coffee was available every two hours. During the day, when he needed me for something he would either ring a bell that was connected to the pantry or have his Orderly deliver a message. After dinner, I was relieved of my duties.

The atmosphere in his dining room was private

and relaxed. There was no socializing, only talk about the ship and its mission. There was never alcohol served while at sea or at port. For cocktail hour, I would serve a fruit cocktail or orange sherbet.

I remember when liquor was discovered on the ship. A couple of sailors were intoxicated and when their lockers were searched pint-sized bottles were found. They were sentenced to 30 days in the brig and were only given bread and water.

One time, while on liberty, I got so drunk I hardly made it back on the ship. I went to my room to lie down but I kept waking up afraid I would find the captain's Orderly standing over my bunk. When that didn't happen, I submitted to my drunk and sunk into a deep sleep. I managed to function for two days, going through the motions, until the "high" wore off. God sure saved me that time.

Laboa and I learned how to prepare breakfast, lunch, and dinner in a pantry that was small but large enough that we hardly touched. There was a stove, a place to store the dishes, a sink, and a few utensils.

Our day began at 0500 and ended at 1830. We would place the food on a plate and then on a large serving tray. There were two waiters assigned to the Captain's Mess, and they were responsible for making sure the plates of food prepared made it to the guest's table. Approximately an hour later, the waiters would pick up the plates and utensils and return them to us.
In between meals, the four of us would polish the sterling silverware that sometimes took three hours. We would wash, rinse, polish and then rinse them again. It was a chore by itself. The captain wanted the silverware to look identical to the ones he used when he dined with royalty.

One winter, while sailing towards Halifax, Novascotia, we entered into a storm. The weather in this area had a tendency to suddenly change. Instead of it settling down, it gained momentum. The captain immediately ordered for everyone to place their life jackets on. The wind was so strong the ship would

In 1947, after serving two years in the United States Navy, my position was Steward, rank was Petty Officer Second Class, and my duties were almost identical to Momma Gussie. I felt like I never left Texas.

weave from the star board side (right) and the port side (left) at a roughly 45 degree angle. I noticed the freezing weather had caused the waters to be whipped into roller coaster whitecaps. I jumped in my bunk and placed the pillow over my head. Suddenly it dawned on me that I couldn't swim. It was prayin' time. There is an old saying in the Navy of how to do things, "The right way, the wrong way, the Navy way, and my way." At this time I added, "And God's way." It was my first near-death experience at sea and it wouldn't be my last. After the storm subsided, I was so confused I didn't know if I should scratch my watch or wind my butt. It took several hours for me to fully recover.

In July 1947, Captain Dauhl was assigned as the new commanding officer on the *Palau* and I was instructed to carry out my duties in the same manner. Dauhl was a lot shorter than Cleaves but his character and confidence made him appear taller. One day, he called me to his office and asked what I thought about accompanying Brigadier General Benjamin O. Davis, Sr.

and his son, Colonel Benjamin O. Davis, Jr., on a special assignment to Liberia. I was so excited I walked away without giving a response, but then I snapped back in line and addressed the Captain appropriately. "It would be the happiest days of my life Captain Sir!"

He said I would be responsible for transporting their luggage to the rooms, unpacking their belongings, hanging up their uniforms, and making sure the wardrobe chosen for the evening was placed at the foot of their beds.

The purpose of the trip was because President Tubman of Liberia wanted to bestow General Davis, Sr. the "Grade of the Commander of the Order of the Star of Africa" award. It was the African country's Centennial Celebration and it was their way of saying thank you to the General for 37 years of support and friendship.

In 1910, the Army assigned General Davis to report the status of Liberia's military duties. He developed a trusting relationship with their dignitaries, and when they visited Washington, D.C. he would accompany them to state dinners, tours, and shows.

I did not sleep a wink that night; I was afraid I would wake up and discover it was all in my mind. I just could not believe that Benjamin Davis, Sr., the first Black General in the United States Army, and Benjamin Davis, Jr., the first Tuskegee Airman licensed and the leader of the unit the Red Tails were actually going to be on the *Palau*. A scuttlebutt was that the Captain spoke in private to a few other Black men about the Davis' visit. It was obvious he wanted to make sure a sufficient number of Black faces were in that greeting line the second they boarded the ship.

The Davis' were known to tour Negro Troops and gather information about the pros and cons of life in the military. They were determined to prove to those who believed that Blacks were of a lower average intelligence were incorrect. They also wanted to better the conditions and improve the race relations between the White and Black soldiers.

When General Davis submitted a proposal to high ranked officials he felt would resolve these issues, he recommended a course in race relations, that no one with a uniform be discriminated against, MPs be properly uniformed, and *all* soldiers be given a course in Black history. He believed that the lack of media coverage of the Black officers was one of the main reasons they were so harshly discriminated against by the general public, and that it was "utterly impossible for any White man to appreciate what the colored officers and soldiers experienced in trying to develop a high morale under present conditions."

As the Davis' boarded the *Palau*, we lined up and saluted. General Davis was the epitome of strength and remained quiet when he walked by the line. But when Colonel Davis walked by he made sure to say a few words.

The Captain acknowledged to the Colonel that I would be the one taking care of them. When he stood in front of me I froze from the strength of his presence.

Brigadier General Benjamin O. Davis, Sr. was the first Black General in the U.S. Army. He was a very kind, quiet man while on the *Palau*.

Colonel Benjamin Davis, Jr. was the commander of the Tuskegee Airman, and the second Black Four-Star General in the U.S. Air Force. When he walked on the *Palau,* he looked more like a Hollywood actor than a Colonel.

He said something to me but I was so in awe I completely blanked out. He was tall with smooth skin with a strong jaw line and deep voice. His uniform looked like it was painted on and his shoes were spit shined. He was of unusual intelligence and fitness, ramrod straight in his posture, and spoke decisively. Colonel Benjamin O. Davis, Jr., was the best looking Black man I had ever seen in my life.

I had three other men from my division to assist me with the Davis' belongings. We walked in front and to clear the way I yelled, "Gang way!" Once they were situated in their rooms, we stood at attention and I asked, "Is there anything else needed Sir?" Colonel Davis said, "No." We saluted and exited the room.

I will never forget the first time I served General Davis a cup of coffee. He asked, "Where are you from son?" My knees buckled then I regained my stance and answered what I was asked only. The General was a quiet man, courteous, and somewhat of a loner. He would pick up a napkin if someone dropped it, always said thank you, and was the first to say good morning. Colonel Davis, on the other hand, spent most of his time where the Captain was stationed-on the bridge observing operations. I served him coffee a few times and retrieved a briefcase and books from his room.

I was a Pollywog because I never crossed the equator and therefore I had to be initiated; a Shellback was someone who had crossed the equator and was already initiated. On the day of this dreadful tradition, the longest standing Shellback was crowned King Neptune, and the next in line with seniority was his messenger, followed by other Shellbacks who were dressed like pirates. They gathered at a presentation table where the King sat in a high-back chair waiting for us poor Pollywogs to kiss his stomach. He had the power to decide if the initiation was going to be punishment or a jail-like sentence. This ritual was meant to toughen up sailors and it was also supposed to gain the support of Neptunes Rex, the god of the sea.

My initiation was punishment and it would be a

day to never be forgotten. Three days of sewage was placed in a snake like tubing, and while I eagerly waited in line for my beating, a chunk of the smelly gook was slapped in the middle of my head. As I crawled through the tube, they pounded my butt, shoulder, head, and ears. I knew God blessed my soul when I made it out of there in one piece. It took longer to get the disgusting smell out of my clothes and hair than it did for my butt to sit in a chair for more than two minutes.

Colonel Davis was a Pollywog and the rules did not exclude high-ranked officials. He was scheduled to endure the same initiation like the one I had just survived. As he crawled on his knees through the tubing he never made a sound. It made the sailors feel like they were weak so they began to hit him like he owed them money. When it was over, he calmly stood up, wiped his sleeves, and touched the top of his head. He gracefully walked over to a water hose and rinsed the gook from his hair and made sure the few out of

In July 1947, on the USS *Palau* CVE-122, Laboa, the Chief Steward of the Captain's Mess, and I were preparing dinner for General Davis, Sr. and Colonel Davis, Jr., while sailing to Monrovia, Liberia.

place strands fell back in line with the others.

The *Palau* docked at a port in Monrovia. Our administration and the Davis' exited the ship and waiting to greet them were the Liberian officials, their leader President Tubman, and a band. General Davis was asked to sing the Liberian National Anthem and although it had been 30 years since he recited the words he remarkably did so perfectly.

After observing this historical moment from the ship's deck, I stayed on board to help Laboa prepare for the private parties and events scheduled to take place over the next two weeks. Once the planning and ordering were complete, I went on Liberty to visit some of the historical sites.

At the last dinner on the ship, which was prepared for President Tubman and military dignitaries, I overheard the officers make negative comments about the speech General Davis gave to the Liberian public. Apparently, the statement given to him on behalf of the United States government was partially replaced with his words. General Davis said that the U.S. promised to extend aid to their country but it depended on what the Liberians would do to help themselves. This point, which was his, caused a little discomfort on both sides. I, on the other hand, became a little nervous watching one of my idols unusually quiet.

When we returned to Norfolk, I received my first "Good Conduct" certificate and was informed a medal would be delivered in approximately four weeks. This recognition was one way the Navy said thank you to those of us who managed to stay out of trouble for two consecutive years.

Almost exactly a year from the day we left for Liberia, on July 20, 1948, General Benjamin Davis, Sr. hung up his uniform after serving 50 years in the Army. President Harry S. Truman attended his retirement party, and on the 26th day of that same month and year, he signed Executive Order 9981 which promised to end segregation in the armed forces and promote equality of treatment and opportunity for all persons regardless of their race, color, religion, and or national origin.

It wasn't until 1971, when the U.S. Navy appointed their first Black admiral. In 1946, Samuel L. Gravely, Jr. was released from active duty and placed on Reserves, but because of Truman's Order he was recalled in 1949. Vice Admiral Gravely was the first Black to achieve Flag Rank in the Navy.

After serving 34 years in the Air Force, Lieutenant General Benjamin Davis, Jr. retired in 1970. On December 9, 1998, President Bill Clinton advanced his rank to a Four-Star General, making him the second to hold that post in the United States Air Force. The first was Daniel "Chappie" James, Jr. and it was President Richard M. Nixon who nominated him in 1975.

General Chappie James, also known by his fellow pilots as the "Black Eagle", learned to fly while attending the Tuskegee Institute. He trained the all-black 99th Pursuit Squardon on how to fly planes while engaged in combat in World War II, excelled in 110

Chappie James stands in front of his fighter jet during the Vietnam War. From 1966-1967, he flew 78 missions. In 1943, Daniel "Chappie" James, Jr. joined the United States Air Force and in 1975 became the first Black Four-Star General. His pilots found it hilarious watching his 6'2, 240 pound frame squeeze out of the cockpit of a fighter jet.

missions assigned to him during the Korean War, and shot down the highest number of MiGs of any mission during the Vietnam War.

When Chappie James walked in a room everyone would stop what they were doing to stare at his awesome presence. He was 6'2 and weighed approximately 240 pounds. Chappie's sense of humor, his ability to articulate and excel in every sport coupled with his "proud to be Black" demeanor opened the doors that he so boldly walked through. He brought new meaning to the old Negro belief, "God made us Black to stand out and that we were different like an apple willing and able to adapt in any environment because we were special."

In spite of a busy schedule, he found time to convey to youth groups and minority students that with desire there was no limit on what they could achieve regardless of the societal pressures and detractors. Chappie believed in order; that it doesn't run you, you have to run it. He also enjoyed smoking cigars when he was in his relaxed mode.

In addition to cooking, cleaning, and serving, I was required to learn the proper loading drills and testing ammunition procedures in case of an emergency. The *Palau* had two five-inch, 38 caliber guns that fired 12-15 rounds per minute. My loading crew consisted of five men; I was the number four relay man.

The first in line would pick up the 53-55 pound bullet out of a wooden crate and pass it on to the man next to him. This is where the old saying "pass the ammunition" was derived from. The fifth man would hand it to the gunners mate in the gun turet. He would then load it into the gun and the other gunners mate would fire it.

After two hours of training, the sound from the numerous rounds of shooting was so loud and piercing, my ears rang for two weeks. The penetration was so disturbing my senses were out of balance and it affected my work but thank God only I could tell the difference.

No one notice my mistakes except for me.

The first time I held the ammunition in my hand, my heart jumped out of my chest and into the bottom of my shoe. I assumed it was detonated, ready to be fired, and when I looked down at the wooden crate box and saw that there were hundreds of them packed side by side, I stopped breathing for a few minutes. I was more than shell shocked, I was devastated.

I remember when a shipmate informed me about the worst disaster in the history of the military, the Port Chicago explosion. On July 17, 1944, on the Port Chicago pier, which was located about 33 miles from San Francisco, California Black seamen were instructed by Black Petty Officers Second Class to load a cargo of bombs that were supposedly defused. At first, they resisted taking orders from the Petty Officers because they looked at them as "Uncle Toms" and "slave drivers", but eventually they formed an assembly line and handled the boxes accordingly. After the last man stacked the boxes in the ship's railcar a bomb detonated causing a ton of ammunition to explode. The two Navy ships, the pier, and major portions of the city were destroyed, 320 seamen and civilians were killed, and approximately 400 were injured.

My Navy buddy Leroy lost his cousin in the Chicago explosion. His family referred to it as "a living nightmare." He said the men were not given gloves to lift the heavy boxes, and the civilians that were hired never received any training. He also said six months later, the Navy had the audacity to order 328 Black sailors to return to the same unsafe conditions to carry out the same duties as the one's given on the day of the Port Chicago disaster, but 258 of the sailors refused. As a result, 208 were given bad conduct discharges and three months without pay, and the remaining 50 were arrested and found guilty of mutiny and given sentences that ranged from five to seventeen years in a federal prison. They were dishonorably discharged which meant they no longer existed. When the Navy escorts you off a ship and out the gate, the only thing you walk out with is your name and the right to vote.

After the war, in 1946, President Harry S. Truman ordered that all men involved in the Port Chicago tragedy receive clemency. Supreme Court Justice Thurgood Marshall, the NAACP Legal Defense Fund Lawyer at that time, spoke on behalf of the Black sailors. He said, "Negroes in the Navy don't mind loading ammunition, they just want to know why they are the only ones doing the loading!"

I later learned I would be required to practice loading on every ship I was assigned to. This additional duty and knowledge of the Port Chicago explosion prompted me to make burial arrangements in case I died while at sea. I requested my remains be brought home but if God forbid, any of us were struck, and body parts were collected here and there, the admiral would decide on the final resting place for the sake of the family.

Loading detonated ammunition was the only command I ever wanted to refuse during my years in the Navy. But I made a commitment when I raised my right hand on the day I was enlisted and said:

> "I, Arby Hambric, do solemnly swear that I will support and defend the Constitution of the United States against all enemies, foreign and domestic; that I will bear true faith and allegiance to the same; and that I will obey the orders of the President of the United States and the orders of the officers appointed over me, according to regulations and the Uniform Code of Military Justice. So help me God."

- - - It is Written - - -

Three

IN THE COMPANY OF MEN PLUS ONE

It was challenging being the only Black sailor on the captain's staff. There were times I felt perplexed and torn and I had no one to share my experiences with. My shipmates were curious about my position but there was little I could say. I wasn't sure if they were sincere or if it was a trap and my comment would get back to the captain.

I decided to dust off my dreams with courage and wisdom and strengthened my sense of hope of one day being more than just a Negro from Centerville. It was wrong of me in the first place to have given up even if it was for a short period of time.

I assumed my position and performed on, what I imagined, the level of a four star restaurant. I remained poised when I felt fatigued and efficient when my thoughts wanted to wonder. I anticipated the captain and his guest's requests before they were needed. I knew who wanted a second serving, who preferred their meat cooked rare, medium, or well-done, when to serve coffee after the main course, and who never wanted desert because of caloric restrictions. After assisting White officers all day, I returned to the separate, segregated quarters, which were slowly-I mean at a snail's pace-integrating.

On June 25, 1950, President Harry S. Truman declared war on People's Republic of North Korea. It was announced on the USS *Palau's* P.A. system and a short summary of what was to be expected was published in the daily "Plan of the Day." Because we were docked at the base in Norfolk, Virginia and classified "safe", we were told not to panic and that we had not received orders to proceed into the war zone. To lessen my anxiety, I continued to write Momma every month. I learned how to concentrate on the opportunities I was afforded and the men I was blessed to be in the company of-both the good and the bad.

During free time on the ship, the Black sailors would mingle to tell lies and stretch the truth. It was their way of getting to know one another. I became acquainted with a newcomer named Carl Brashear. We had a lot in common except for one major thing; he could swim and I couldn't tread water.

Carl was a Steward but when he arrived on the *Palau* he was classified a Motor Whaleboat Coxswain-Deck Division, and his duties were to clean and maintain the deck. He was from Tonieville, a small town in Kentucky that no one ever heard of and he dropped out of school to work in the fields with his family.

I remember how fascinated he was watching a diver retrieve a plane that had rolled off the flight deck of the *Palau* and into the ocean. He said that one day he was going to become a diver and would be the best they had ever seen. I supported his idea, but then I got to thinking that maybe he was one of those guys who were the exception to the rule. When he was reassigned to another ship, I knew there was more to come from him. I counted on his defense of courage and determination to outsmart the opposition.

In 1954, I learned that Carl became the first Black

to graduate from the U.S. Navy Diving & Salvage School. In 1960, at the age of 29, he received his GED, and in 1970, he became the first to become a Master Diver in the U.S. Navy. In 2000, famed actor Cuba Gooding, Jr. portrayed his life in the blockbuster movie, "Men of Honor." Carl Brashear believed that it wasn't a sin to get knocked down it was a sin to stay down.

The purpose of the United States entering the Korean War was to end a possible invasion of South Korea, a free world, by North Korea, a communist country. Truman feared the Soviets would try to take over "one by one" and gain power and therefore the military was advised to contain all and any communist expansionism. In December of that same year, President Truman was scheduled to visit the *Palau* for reasons that were not leaked whatsoever.

On the day of his arrival, we were instructed to man the rail until he came on board the ship. The temperature was nine degrees; it was the coldest morning I ever experienced during my service in the

Navy and the skivvies I wore did nothing to block the cold wind from blowing through my pants. My butt cheeks were frozen and my fingers felt like icicles.

We were instructed to remain at parade rest while Truman inspected the other ships in the area. The Navy's idea of being on time is to "hurry up and wait." One hour later, he walked up the steps and on board appearing larger than life. We stood at attention and when he walked by I gave a slanted salute that was somewhat on point. All I could think about was how proud Momma would have been to see her cotton-picking son in the presence of such a great man. It would be one of the most honorable and memorable days of them all.

While stationed on the *Palau*, I learned how to tolerate those who were considered "bad." Theophilus Eugene "Bull" Connor was a racist bigot who believed in segregation at all costs. His cousin, whose first name I chose to forget and face I would never, was as hard on Black sailors as Bull was on civil right activists.

Carl Brashear (back row second right) decided to become a diver when he was assigned on the USS *Palau*. The only thing we didn't have in common was he knew how to swim and I didn't. In 1970, he became the first Black Master Diver in the United States Navy.

During the early 1960s, Bull Connor was the public safety officer for Birmingham, Alabama. When activists in the Civil Rights Movement marched down the streets of Birmingham, Bull was supposed to protect them from the angry mob of people and members of the Klu Klux Klan, but instead he directed the fire departments and policemen to use high-pressured fire hoses and dogs to force them to leave town. What Bull failed to realize was that a television cameraman and a photographer with *Life* magazine was capturing the horrific turn of events. President John F. Kennedy as well as the majority of people from all races was infuriated. This moment in history would be the spark that would lead Kennedy to sign the Civil Rights Act of 1964.

Bull Connor's cousin was a Boatswain Mate on the *Palau*, which was like a policeman without a gun. He was oddly tall and stout, and had a reputation of carrying a big stick. His duty was to arrest a sailor and place him in the brig. A jail sentence could range from three to ten days with three meals, or the most severe, 30 days with only bread and water. When we found out he was giving only water to Black sailors with light sentences, word began to spread like a tornado through a trailer park. The captain corrected the problem quickly and sent Bull Connor's cousin sailing elsewhere.

On the *Palau*, we definitely had our share of Jim Crow tactics and gestures. But I always found it strange that when the men of all races got together to play poker, racism and prejudice were never present.

In June 1951, I was transferred from the USS *Palau* to FASRON 108-VP7, a patrol squadron at the Naval Air Station Quonset Point in Quonset Point, Rhode Island. I settled in the barracks and wrote a letter to Momma so she would know where I was stationed. I placed a crisp $5 dollar bill inside and after I sealed it, I kissed her name three times.

One night, I stood on the deck leaning against the rail and gazing at the full moon. I thought about what I left back home and what could possibly be waiting in front of me. Then a strong breeze blew my hat off and into a corner. Instead of rushing to recover it, I adhered to a sense of calm. The idea of settling down hit me between the eyes, and that could only mean one thing.

My church friends had introduced me to a young lady named Alma Harrison when I was stationed in Norfolk. She was a sweet, petite 17 year old and I was 25. After courting for two months I found myself thinking about her quite often.

I moved into a two bedroom military house that was located off the Quonset Point base but was nearby. After I purchased a few necessities, I called Alma and said there was something I wanted to ask her and that I would send money for a bus ticket. For the first time in my life, I was ready, willing, and able.

One late evening after dinner, in my own poetic country fashion, I flopped down on both of my knees and handed her a little square box with a red rose and proposed. She accepted without hesitation. I was so excited I near 'bout stood on my head. Alma wanted to live in different parts of the world and the move to Rhode Island was what she envisioned the life of a sailor's wife would be like.

During the day, I reported to duty on the base, and after putting in eight hours I reported back home. On the way, I occasionally stopped at the "watering hole" to share war stories and tell lies about the women I met along the way with my sailor buddies, and to reacquaint myself with my long-time friend, the scotch whiskey, Johnny Walker. We sailors brought a new refined meaning to its slogan, "Wherever ships could sail."

Every so often, I was asked to put in late hours. When Alma became anxious and uncomfortable with the idea of being in a house alone especially at night, we decided this would be the perfect time to have a child. On June 8, 1952, our first child was born, Arby Hambric, Jr., and our relationship was more solid and steady. I could only hope it would fill the void and alleviate at least some of her fears.

That same year, my squadron was assigned to the FASRON 108-VP7 mission for the United States Pacific Fleet, a six month deployment at the Iwakuni Air Force Base in Iwakuni, Japan. The country was in the midst of the Korean War and it was no longer between the North and South now the United Nations and China had entered the picture. What began as a war between two countries was now international. I still wasn't worried about the possible dangers even though it would be the closest I came to direct combat. What was troubling me was whether or not Alma would understand that I had to react immediately when called to duty. I found enough courage to tell her the news. She remained calm but deep down inside she was disturbed.

When we I arrived in Japan, I never saw that many naval vessels in one body of water in my life. I was assigned to be the Steward for the commanding officer and his squadron, VP 7. My duty was to serve coffee and sandwiches Monday thru Friday from 7:00

a.m. to 4:00 p.m. The commander was responsible for reconnaissance flights and enemy surveillance and his headquarters was set up at the squadron's hanger.

Then news traveled throughout the military that President Harry S. Truman relieved Five-Star General Douglas MacArthur from his duties for insubordination. Now I was worried. MacArthur felt it was necessary to extend the conflict into China; President Truman did not. Although they had a conflict of views, what I gathered from the table discussions in the Captain's Mess was that President Truman wanted to convey a message to the world that he was the commander-in-chief and no one had the authority to question his orders. There was a sign on his desk that read "The Buck Stops Here" and that's exactly what he meant when he replaced General MacArthur with General Matthew Ridgeway in April 1951.

The Korean War ended on July 27, 1953. After three years of fighting and five million lives lost, 40,000 were Americans, we failed to unify the country. The government classified this war period in our history as the Korean Police Action.

It was a hot and humid day and I was so desperate to cool down I dove off a spring board and into a swimming pool on the Iwakuni Air Force base. The next thing I remember was waking up in the base dispensary. The doctor said I blacked out the second I hit the water and was unconscious for quite some time. He added that I was nothing short of a miracle and if it wasn't for the immediate reaction of a sailor I would have drowned. The sailor who saved my life was in my unit. His last name was Hollinsworth and he was the nicest White guy I ever had the pleasure of getting to know. I made peace with my silly behavior and accepted that swimming is not a skill that comes natural. Momma said the next time I can't stand the heat buy an ice cream cone.

I completed the FASRON mission and was informed that my next assignment, FAW-3 squadron, would take me back to the Naval Air Station Quonset

When President Harry S. Truman's (left) relieved Five-Star General Douglas MacArthur from his command in the midst of the Korean War that's when I started to get nervous.

President Harry S. Truman's (left) and Fleet Admiral William D. Leahy on the USS *Sarsfield* in 1951. Admiral Leahy was the first naval officer to hold a Five-Star rank in the U.S. Armed Forces. He was opposed to Truman's atomic bomb because he felt no war could be won by destroying women and children.

Point in Quonset Point, Rhode Island. I was assigned to Captain Argyll E. Buckley and his family-wife and two children. They resided on the base and my duty was similar to the ones I carried out on a ship. I prepared three meals a day, and when it was necessary to run an errand or go shopping for groceries, I had access to the Captain's car and his personal driver.

Captain Buckley was related to editor, author, commentator, and television personality, William F. Buckley, Jr. Among one of his many heroic achievements was utilizing his magazines and collected writings to define the boundaries of conservatism. On numerous occasions, Mr. Buckley came for dinner. He and the Captain would spend the entire time, from the second he walked in the door, talking about politics, military strategies, and government affairs. He was a serious minded young man and I often wondered if he ever got any sleep.

Alma was happy I was home. On my days off, which were normally Saturday and Sunday, she planned family outings. It was her way of strengthening our bond that she claimed weakened every time I left on assignment. It was also a subtle way to get closer to my son Arby Jr. It was obvious there was distance between us.

I wanted to look at my son in the eyes and feel a connection but there was something missing. I was lost for words and awkward in my response towards him. I didn't want to lean on the excuse of growing up without a father, but what else could it be. I questioned my role and my capability, and because I had no answers, I continued to do what I learned in the Navy- to act accordingly.

After I completed my shift on the base, I started stopping by a "watering hole" my shipmates frequented. Alma complained that I was drinking too much. Instead of admitting my guilt, I caved in and promised to stop, but the only change I made was my "watering" schedule and an increased purchase of Listerine mouthwash.

My next transfer was in 30 days, and I would report to the Philadelphia Naval Shipyard. It was the country's first shipyard. I was a little nervous being stationed there because I heard about the mystery of the "Philadelphia Experiment", officially called "Project Rainbow" that was launched in 1943 on the USS *Aldrige*. The experiment was to find the difference between space and time, and the mission was to make the ship invisible to the radar and naked eye so it would disappear when sailing from Norfolk Harbor and reappear in Philadelphia. It was said that of the 180 crew, 120 were missing and 40 were said to have been dead. This experiment was "officially denied" even though claims were filed on the dead seamen.

When I told Alma the news, she flipped out and mentioned the sacrifices she has made just to be with me. That's when I realized she was homesick and painfully missing her friends. We sat down and agreed she and Arby Jr. should move back home to Norfolk, and that I would send money every month and see them when I could. After careful thought about this arrangement, I felt that since I was practically "married" to the Navy it would only be fair to give her the freedom to live her life as she saw fit. I contacted a reputable attorney in Teague, Texas, and informed him that I wanted to file for a divorce and continue my monthly payments of support.

After reporting for duty, I learned that I would be solely responsible for the captain's staff and I would be assigned an assistant. This bit of news was good but alarming. I also discovered that I would be on a ship instead of the shipyard. In other words, my current personal affairs and new assignment was causing a lot of butterflies in my stomach.

One cloudy afternoon aboard a dry docked ship (her name I can't recall) on the Naval Shipyard, I was cleaning the pantry in the Captain's Mess when the messenger handed me a letter. It was from Alma's attorney. She filed for an increase of child support and I knew it was her revengeful way of getting back at me for wanting a divorce. According to my attorney in Texas, there was nothing I could do or say. I felt hopeless and vulnerable, and silly as it sounds, I understood her reasons for wanting more. It's what we all want. She felt like she had paid a price and here was the bill. I made arrangements with the Navy's finance department to have a percentage of my monthly salary, which at the time was $300, to be sent to her until Arby Jr. was 18 years of age.

In between my excursions with Johnny Walker, I stopped avoiding the fact that although I didn't take marriage seriously I thought she would never leave. I carried on with a smile but I felt like a failure, and that my chances of finding a soul-mate were slim to none. That old, tired miserable feeling lingered, but I commanded it to leave. Uncle Henry used to say, "Living in worry invites death in a hurry." I wasn't ready for that, not yet.

Captain Dunlap was assigned to the ship. My duties were to prepare two square meals (breakfast and lunch) for his staff and guests. My assistant would take care of the staff's state rooms. He was getting close to retirement and thought that a sit down dinner would allow him to network and prove to be beneficial in the long run. He asked if I would cook something special for a "few good men."

I prepared roast beef brisket. It was so tender and thinly sliced to perfection one of the guests became overly excited. He stood and looked at me and said, "Leave the Navy immediately and I could make you a rich man!"

In my two years, on this particular ship, I had the pleasure of being under the leadership of two great captains. However, the one I was personally acquainted with was Jeremiah Andrew Denton, Jr.

At the time, Captain Denton's principal field of endeavor was naval operations. His career included being stationed on a variety of ships, aircraft, and airships, also referred to as blimps. Like Dunlap, Denton's headquarters were set up on the ship. A few times, I went out of my way to greet him and in return he made time for a private discussion. We talked about scriptures in the Bible, what they meant, and how to apply the message in our daily lives. He appreciated it when I blessed his food with a prayer of gratitude. For someone who was so heavily involved with confidential missions, it was a pleasure to know that he was a humble man with a strong belief in God.

In May 1956, two weeks prior to his departure, Captain Denton informed me that I was being re-assigned to the Pacific Reserve Fleet in Long Beach, California. He insisted we bow our heads and say a prayer. When he was finished, I knew everything was going to be okay. I learned later that Captain Jeremiah Denton received acclaimed recognition for his revolutionary "Haystack Concept" which proved that it was safer for ships to sail solo than with a fleet.

When I arrived on the Long Beach Naval Shipyard in Long Beach, California, I instantly fell in love with the weather. It was picture perfect and I only needed a light jacket when the sun went down. The Naval Shipyard was where the training headquarters for fleet patrolling and escorting took place. My assignment was Desflot-1, which was an abbreviation for Destroyer Flotilla. My rank was still Petty Officer Second Class but after I checked in for duty, I was surprised to learn that I was promoted to serve on the admiral's staff. This meant that I was responsible for overseeing the operations concerning the kitchen and state rooms, and assigned three assistants to help prepare and serve the food.

My responsibilities would be similar to that of the captain's staff except I would assist the needs of his staff which normally consisted of approximately seven officers. I wasn't required to do the housework or laundry-the assistants took care of these chores. I felt like I was moving up in the world. Of all the fleet of vessels, I felt proud and honored that I would be on the one that was considered the flagship which meant it was the largest, fastest, and most heavily armed of them all. Even so, I was nervous working in the kitchen. The food was required to be on the table when it was warm enough to consume and the desert was served as soon as the main course was over. The captain required this perfectly timed service, but this was the admiral, the top dog, and I sure wouldn't want an unfavorable report from him.

When I prepared the dessert, Baked Alaska, I would sweat bullets. After the ice cream was frozen between the layers of cake, I would beat the egg whites by hand until soft peaks formed, added sugar and beat until the meringue was stiff and glossy. I would then pour the mixture over the entire cake and place it in a 400 degree oven until the meringue was a light brown color. As soon as I took the dessert out of the oven, I could only pray that the admiral and his staff were willing, able, and ready for consumption.

In July 1957, the Vietnam War was underway, and I was assigned on the CRUDIV-5 (cruiser division) USS *Los Angeles* CA-135, on the San Diego Naval

In 1956, I was stationed at the Long Beach Naval Shipyard. We were returning on the bus after a little recreation.

Entertainer, Danny Kaye (center) walked off the stage after his performance to say hello and thank you. We were in Melbourne, Australia for the 1956 *XVI Olympics*.

While stationed on the USS *Los Angeles* CA-135, I was the Senior Steward for Admiral John Davidson's staff.

In 1957, on the heavy duty cruiser, USS *Los Angeles* CA-135. Front, center on both pictures, I was the only Black chosen from my division to serve on the admiral's staff.

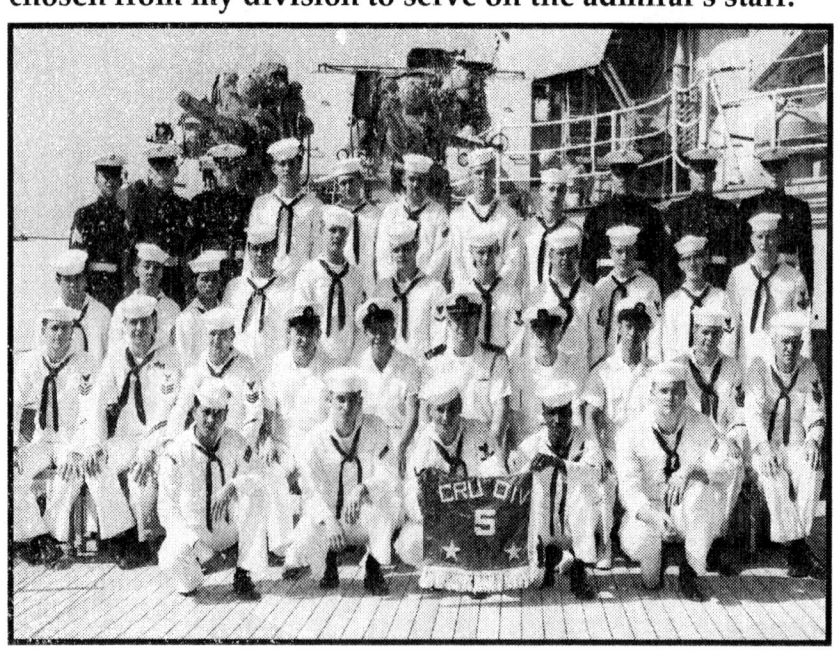

Shipyard in San Diego, California, and was promoted as the Senior Steward on Admiral John Davidson's staff.

After working a few months in my new position, I felt comfortable with the services I was required to provide and the surroundings. I decided to hang out at a watering hole to throw back a few scotch & sodas and talk trash with the fellas. I turned to laugh at a corny joke when I noticed an attractive young lady sitting at a table with a "girl" friend. I put down my drink and walked over to introduce myself. Her name was Veronica Pinkstonia and she was from Nashville, Tennessee. She had recently moved to San Pedro, California, which was located within driving distance.

From the moment she said that first hello, I knew I was going to somehow, someway, end up with her by the end of the day. She was a little broad in the beam, and I sure wanted to warm up to those buns. It is so funny how the quality and character of a woman can bring a sense of peace and comfort to a man.

On our first date, I found out she was recently

divorced. Her husband was a longshoreman who did the wrong things at the wrong time and it caused them to lose their house. She had a problem with trust and I knew I had to do some convincing in order for our relationship to move forward.

Our first test came sooner than I expected. I was informed that my next assignment was WESTPAC, which involved sailing across the western Pacific Ocean for an unspecified amount of time on the CRUDIV-5 USS *Los Angeles* CA-135. When I broke the news to her she was very understanding. That's when I knew she was what we men call "a keeper."

Even though I was the only Black sailor on the admiral's staff, I still had to sleep in the Steward's quarters, which remained separate and segregated but mostly by choice-some of us were more comfortable being around our own kind. Veronica and I wrote each other every week. I talked about my experiences on the ship and she bragged about her winnings at the dog races in Tijuana, Mexico. She mentioned her family quite a bit and her future plans which did not include a husband or so it seemed. I admitted how lonely it was being out at sea for four to six months, and I purposely did not write one word about the Vietnam War because as far I knew we were not instructed to sail inside the war zone.

After serving two years on the CRUDIV-5 USS *Los Angeles,* I received a letter typed in capital letters from Admiral Hopwood commending me on my service. It read:

I AM PARTICULARLY GRATIFIED TO NOTE THE OUTSTANDING RECORD YOU HAVE SET DURING YOUR TOUR IN WESTPAC. ONE OF THE PRIME MISSIONS OF OUR DEPLOYED UNITS IS THE PROMOTION OF INTERNATIONAL GOOD WILL IN FOREIGN LANDS. AS DIPLOMATS OF THE U.S. NAVY AND THE ENTIRE COUNTRY, YOU HAVE BY YOUR OUTSTANDING CONDUCT AND EXAMPLE PERFORMED THIS MISSION IN

A MOST EXEMPLARY MANNER. TO THE COMMANDING OFFICER AND THE ENTIRE CREW OF THE USS LOS ANGELES WELL DONE AND SMOOTH SAILING. ADM. H. G. HOPWOOD

Then in small caps, he added these two points. One stated, "Commander Cruiser Division Five considers that your own perfect conduct record and performance of duty contribute materially to the flagship having been awarded this commendatory message." Secondly, he stated, "In addition, particular notice is taken of your willing sacrifice of personal liberty while assisting in entertaining official guests through the cruise. You are therefore commended for your leadership, personal example, and devotion to this command and the United States Navy." He closed with his personal signature.

I felt honored Admiral Hopwood took time to write a letter about my services and attitude. It was the spark my sense of hope needed, the words my ears needed to hear.

In September 1961, I was assigned on the CRUDESFLOT-7 USS *Helena* CA-75, a heavy cruiser, and a year later, I was assigned on the USS *Piedmont* AD-17, a destroyer tender. Both ports were at the San Diego Naval Shipyard. I took advantage of this time and thought about settling down with Veronica. By now, she knew the difference between a longshoreman and a Navy seaman and that was important.

We had a private marriage ceremony at our new home with only a few close friends from her church and my division present. For our honeymoon, we drove to Tijuana, Mexico, and found ourselves practically living at the Greyhound dog racing track.

Upon my return, I was informed that I was re-assigned to WESTPAC on the USS *Piedmont* for nine months. Before I told Veronica, I went to the Navy headquarters and requested a transfer. I was told the only way that would be approved was if I found a suitable replacement. One of my shipmates, a Filipino,

Steward First Class, volunteered for the assignment. The Pacific Fleet accepted him but Commander Lachocotte, the man in charge of the entire supply department on the *Piedmont,* did not approve it.

Veronica handled the news of my re-assignment like a champ, but even still she was human. Nine months was a long time when you're home alone and when you are out at sea it seems like eternity. I went down to the animal shelter and adopted a four-month old puppy. It was a Chihuahua mixed with Terrier and she was sweet and feisty just like Veronica. She named her Cheetah. Now I was ready to sail.

While the *Piedmont* was anchored in the middle of the Pacific Ocean, I felt empty and distressed. The thought of returning home was so far removed from my mind I couldn't even visualize myself walking in the front door. Veronica continued to write weekly and I wrote words of encouragement even though I felt quite the opposite.

My next assignment, COMTRA PAC, was at the

Naval San Diego Base headquarters. I was on a "Tour of Duty" and to my surprise I was scheduled to be the Senior Steward for my former admiral, John Davidson.

On the home front in San Diego, matters on the outside started to unravel. My wife's best friend, who relocated from Long Beach, was starting to become overly jealous of our relationship. She always wanted to "land" a sailor but never got to first base. My wife told her she wanted to remain friends-at a distance-and that she had other priorities, but that was like talking to a bucket of rocks. When I was at work, she would park in front of the house and approach Veronica when she walked outside. This strange behavior frightened her. There was an old quote that often appeared in various forms on ships. It said, "We can't direct the wind, but we can adjust the sails." Before something terrible happened, I decided to leave the area.

I informed Admiral Davidson about the entire matter and asked if I could be transferred. He put in the order and in less than a month, I was stationed at

Naval Air Station Moffett Field, which was later renamed the Moffett Federal Airfield, located in Santa Clara County near the southern tip of the San Francisco Bay.

Veronica fell in love with the area and the weather. We lived in San Bruno and later found a modest sized house in San Jose. I didn't care that it took 30 minutes to get to work I just wanted to do what was required of me to make her happy. Besides, I did not know how to drive a car, not yet, and I knew this was the perfect time to start learning.

For the past three years, I hitchhiked to work. Around 4:00 a.m., I would stand on the freeway with my uniform on and thumb out. In a matter of seconds someone would stop and offer me a ride. Most people would volunteer even if they weren't going in my direction. They simply wanted to show their appreciation for my service in the military.

When I was home, Veronica trusted me enough to use her car to practice. I would drive and park on the streets in the neighborhood. I knew I was ready to take the exam and the test when I was able to parallel park without having to back up and redo it.

In August 1963, I was given a two-year assignment on the AIR TRAN RON VR-8 Squadron at Moffett Field. After completing one year and seven months, my wife Veronica was diagnosed with ovarian cancer. Thoughts of hanging up my sailor hat hit me right between the eyes. I figured I had lost my first wife from being at sea too often, at least I thought that was the reason of our demise, and I refused to make another conscious mistake even though the circumstances were different. It would be hard to walk away knowing I had three more months on my assignment. Momma raised me to finish whatever I started, but this time I had to turn my back on what I was taught and do what I felt was right.

We were in the midst of the Vietnam War. The United States and South Vietnam attempted to stop the spreading of communism by engaging in battle with the

On the USS *Los Angeles* CA-135. I was awarded the "Good Conduct" certificate by the admiral of the Cruiser Division 5 Staff. It was the third of the six medals I would receive during my 20 years of service in the Navy.

North Vietnamese and Viet Cong, but the military had lost the support of the people because no one felt we could win. The casualty claims filed had increased fifty times the normal rate and they needed to be processed as soon as possible. I always felt that the month of March represented forward progress so on March 1, 1965, I filed the documents to officially retire from the United States Navy. It was the right move at the right time because the next day claims submitted for retirement were "frozen."

On my DD214, the following categories were completed: Rank-Steward First Class; Character of Service-Honorable; Type of Discharge-Release to Inactive Duty; The Highest Civilian Education Level-10 High School; and Race-Negro. It wasn't until 1969, that we had the option to list our race as being Negro, Black, or American.

In July 1965, I learned that Captain Jeremiah Denton's plane was shot down during the Vietnam War by the North Vietnamese. He was captured,

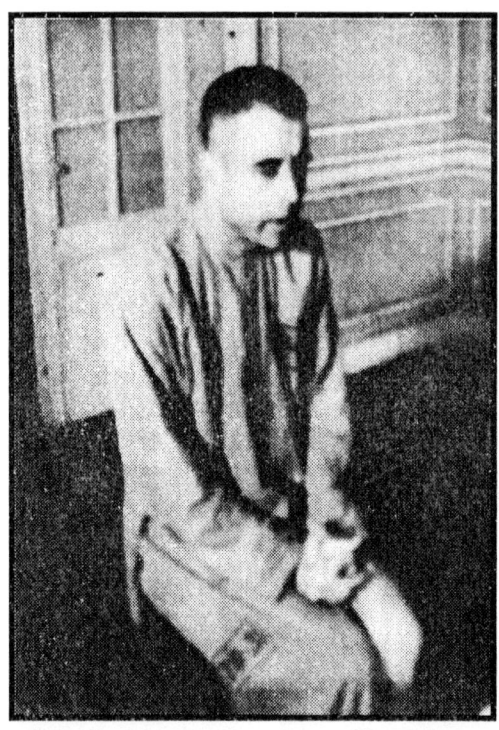

On July 18, 1965, Captain Jeremiah Denton was shot down from his plane and captured by the Viet Cong. By blinking the word torture in Morse code during a press conference resulted in the release of the American P.O.W.s. on February 13, 1973.

In 1977, Jeremiah Denton was promoted to Rear Admiral. He served in World War II, Korea, and Vietnam, and oversaw operations on numerous ships including one I was stationed on at the Philadelphia Naval Yard. He had a strong faith in God.

imprisoned, and tagged a Prisoner of War (P.O.W.) then starved and tortured. I prayed for a miracle and I was sure he did as well.

The Viet Cong wanted the American P.O.W.s to admit that they committed war crimes against North Vietnam and to reveal U.S. military secrets. Captain Jeremiah Denton capitalized on the opportunity to use a press conference he knew would be viewed by the U.S. Office of the Navy Intelligence. He looked straight into the camera and talked with a high-pitched voice, and at the same time, blinked in Morse code the letters T O R T U R E. It was the ammunition the United States Military needed to proceed with a plan of action.

From December 19-29, 1972, Hanoi and Haiphong were bombed, destroying the buildings and villages surrounding the camps. This mission became known as the "Christmas Bombings" and its results lead to peace talks and eventually the release of the American P.O.W.s. On February 12, 1973, during "Operation Homecoming", one of the first prisoners to walk off the plane at Clark Air Base on Philippine soil was Captain Jeremiah Denton. In 1977, the Navy promoted him to Rear Admiral.

In his autobiography, "When Hell Was In Session", he said, "The strength of our nation is more than a material strength. We are a strongly moral people, and our country is based on spiritual strength. Lose that and we lose everything."

What I found peculiar about the public's knowledge of the Vietnam War was the lack of media coverage about the Black POWs who survived. I was only made aware of two by my shipmates otherwise I would be clueless. They were Fred V. Cherry and James A. Daly.

In 1965, Major Cherry became the first Black P.O.W. When his F-105 Thunderbird fighter-bomber was shot down the ejection from his plane caused him to sustain life-threatening injuries. He was placed in a Hanoi prison camp, tortured for 93 days, and spent 53 consecutive weeks in solitary confinement. To destroy what little hope he may have had, Viet Cong moved Navy Lieutenant Porter Halyburton, a White Southerner from Davidson, North Carolina, into his living quarters. Major Cherry was from Suffolk, Virginia, which is about 20 miles from Norfolk. The combination was sure to fail, but as fate had it, the response between the two men was just the opposite. Major Cherry's wounds became so infected, Lt. Halyburton hand fed him and slowly nursed him back to health. It was their strong bond and friendship that kept them from going insane.

After serving seven and a half years in a prison camp, they were released in 1973. At a press conference, Major Fred V. Cherry boldly professed that he would be forever grateful to the man who saved his life, his friend Lt. Porter Halyburton.

Moments after addressing the media, however, Major Cherry learned that everything he lived for vanished. When he went home he discovered that his wife Shirley had left and taken their four children along

In 1973, Major Cherry was the first Black P.O.W. captured and released. Shortly after this photo was taken he discovered that his wife emptied his bank accounts and left him without any knowledge of how to reach her.

In 1973, the Viet Cong purposely placed Lt. Porter Halyburton in the hut with Major Cherry to hopefully cause racial tensions, but instead they became very close friends.

with his life savings. While he was rotting in a prison camp, she received his salary and various allowances until 1970. To stick the knife even further in his back, he discovered she had a child by another man and used his money to pay for the medical expenses.

In 1968, Private First Class James A. "Jim" Daly was captured after his unit was ambushed and sent to a Hanoi prison camp. Daly never wanted to join the military. He did not want to carry a loaded gun nor did he want to pull the trigger because he believed that it was better to be killed than to kill someone. He was a Jehovah Witness and their doctrine did not support violence. He tried to be dismissed from the military based on religion, but they drafted him anyway. A recruiter knew about his beliefs and promised he would serve in non-combat assignments. Shortly after he was enlisted, the war in Vietnam broke out and Daly was sent to fight.

In his biography, "Black Prisoner of War: A Conscientious Objector's Vietnam Memoir", Daly wrote about the Vietnamese and their daily practice of racist tactics. Viet Cong assumed that Southern Whites in particular wanted nothing to do with Blacks and that they would rather starve to death than to consider them as their equal. Although the camps were segregated, Black soldiers were shown favoritism to create distrust among the Whites.

Private Daly was a big man, and his skin color was a blend of coffee with cream. He was the first veteran to expose some of the military tactics during the Vietnam period. He said that for every dead Vietnamese, a G.I. earned a three-day off pass and it didn't matter who or what just as long as it was of their race. He grossly and thoroughly wrote how the body-count system of Americans was enough to make you insane. As a P.O.W., Daly joined the camp's Peace Committee which required each member to sign a letter that opposed the war. He became a controversial figure among veterans and was officially charged, but later cleared upon his release in 1973. After 20 years of fighting and millions of lives lost, the U.S. government did not classify Vietnam as a war, but as a Conflict.

I came to a few conclusions, one in particular, after serving 20 years in the Navy. And that is, when war is declared you can best believe that no matter what reason the government gives somewhere in that picture is a desire to confiscate the enemy's natural resource.

- - - It is Written - - -

Four

★
WINDS OF CHANGE

It was 1966 and I had been officially retired from the U.S. Navy for a year, but my civilian life continued to have remnants of my days on a ship. I woke up at 4:00 a.m. and had no idea what to do at that time of the morning. I learned to stay in bed and force myself to go back to sleep until 7:00 a.m., which was the time Veronica started doing things around the house. I prepared two meals a day, and I was forever grateful to eat at a table instead of standing up in a pantry. I smiled while going through this adjustment. It wasn't easy but I knew it would only last for a short period of time.

One day, while grocery shopping, I bumped into two sailors. I introduced myself and talked about my years in the service. They nodded but had no specific questions for me. When I got in the car, I wept. I missed the ships, the fellas, and the feel of being part of something that mattered to the world. I felt that all those years would go down the drain and my years of service would never be missed by anyone including myself.

I went to work for Sears Roebuck & Co. as a janitor. I was promoted to sales in the automotive division and then as a clerk in shipping and receiving. At that time, in San Jose, California, companies hired military personnel on the spot. If there were no jobs one was created, and if it was frozen they had to reopen it.

Veronica was feeling better. The cancer was in remission and she swore it was because the Shaklee natural products helped her to fight the cancer. I invested a lot of money in the supplements and I even started selling them to balance the costs. I worked around the clock and the only time I slept was on my lunch break at Sears. I wanted so much for these long hours I was putting in outside my regular job to pay off in the end. The least I could do was try and save her life.

I enjoyed her family, especially her favorite cousin, Howard Hill; he was a hoot to hang out with.

He served four years in the Air Force and fought in the Korean War. Howard was intelligent and smart and I admired how he worked during the day and attended college at night to complete his degree in business administration even though it took him 15 years to complete.

In 1956, Howard started working for a post office which was located in a beautiful all-White suburban area called, Compton, California. He started in the mailroom and over a span of 10 years was promoted as the Pacific Palisades Postmaster. He oversaw all operations and was responsible for the mail distribution in Beverly Hills and various other elite areas.

I remember when Howard told me about the changes he went through when he was trying to buy a house in Compton. His paperwork was completed and G.I. Bill was approved. He was anxious to buy but the banks denied his application, and every application, and every real estate agent he contacted did not know of a house for sale. But as fate had it, one day, a co-

Veronica (middle) with cousins Howard Hill (right) and Bunnie Hill (left). Howard and the three men kneeling fought in the Korean War and were just discharged after serving four years (1951-1955) in the U.S. Air Force.

Howard Hill was the Postmaster at the Compton Post Office. His was the first or second Black family to own a home in Compton, a once all-White suburban area.

worker was planning to retire and said he would be happy to sale his house to him. Howard and his wife jumped at the chance. When they purchased it, they became the first—or to be on the safe side-second Black family to move in the neighborhood. Howard said as soon as they placed the couch in the living room, "For Sale" signs started showing up on just about every block. Today, 32.1% of the residents in Compton are Black, .08% White, and the remaining are Hispanics.

I was proud of Veronica's family, as I was of mine. She noticed I talked a little about Teague, Texas, nothing about Centerville, and much about Momma. She was curious about the areas I grew up in and was anxious to visit all of them. When I told her it had been 14 years since I had been home she could not believe it. I didn't waste time giving any explanation. I simply gave my approval of the plans she wanted to make as long it involved driving and not flying. I wanted to make a stop in Phoenix, Arizona, to say hello to the man who saved my life in Japan, my dearest shipmate,

Lieutenant Commander Hollingsworth.

I was hesitant to return home because I was tired of lying to people I cared about just to protect the Navy and to give an impression that I was so much better off in the military than at home. I tried to make peace with this internal battle but no matter how many beds I made, coffee I served, and brisket I prepared, I knew I would be nothing more than a Steward in the Navy. I placed my shame inside the lining of my uniform which was hanging in the back of my closet and thought deeply about my wife. It wasn't about medals or ranks anymore it was about the life we would plan together.

I was ready to see my family like never before. And as I expected, they fell in love with Veronica as she did with them. I hardly recognized the house. With the money I had been sending home, Momma added a bedroom, a laundry room, a carport, and a front porch. She painted the exterior a bright yellow to match her beautiful flowers that perfectly framed the front entrance.

Momma and Charlie were so happy to see us they made the house feel like Christmas. For breakfast, she prepared cream of wheat, scrambled eggs, homemade biscuits with Brer Rabbit Blackstrap Molasses. Oh happy day! I ate so much I had to adjust my belt.

Family members came by to say a few words. It was good to see them especially Uncle A.B. McAdam, my mother's brother, even though he was up to his same old tricks. He finally eased his way in front of me, leaned down, and whispered, "Hey Arby, give me some of that good stuff", but unfortunately my response was not what he wanted to hear. He too was a friend of Johnny Walker and I had decided-for obvious reasons- to leave the liquid gold in the liquor stores. They called him "Mr. Mac" and he was the father of seven children and a deacon at a church in Corsicana, Texas, which was about 34 minutes from the house.

My sisters were grown, gone, and married. Mildred, the youngest, was "joined at the hip" to husband, Ernest Busby, a deacon at a church in Waco, Texas. Busby served 28 years in the Air Force, and in 1946 he played baseball in the semi-professional league for his division. His team would play in tournaments and exhibition games, and sometimes notable players would stop by just to show off their superior talent.

I will never forget the day he told us how he kind of sort of swung and hit a ball thrown by Leroy "Satchel" Paige. In 1948, at the age of 42, Satchel joined the Cleveland Indians and became the first Black pitcher to play in Major League Baseball. He continued to volunteer on semi-pro teams to increase their attendance. He was what they called a "gate attraction" and was known all over the world to be a "special guest" on any semi-pro team he wanted to play on even if it was for just a few innings.

Busby stood about 5'4. He said when he walked up to the plate and looked at Satchel, a tall, dark lanky man displaying funny facial expressions and cracking jokes, his vision blurred. All Busby wanted to do was

My brother-in-law, Ernest Busby played on a semi-pro team for his Air Force division. He said one of the proudest moments in his life was being struck out by Satchel Paige. When 42 year old Leroy "Satchel" Paige made his debut in major league baseball in 1948, he became the first Black pitcher and the oldest rookie to play in major league baseball.

hit a piece of the ball, but it flew by so fast he didn't see it until after it landed in the catcher's mitt. After the third pitch he was baffled; it was one ball and two strikes. But on the fourth pitch he decided to swing no matter what and to his surprise he hit the tip of the ball but it landed in the stands. The next pitch he swung and struck out. On his way to the dugout all he could think about was that he actually hit a ball thrown by the great Satchel Paige. He was overwhelmed with pride and for a long time he thought he was something special.

Leroy Robert Paige earned his nickname Satchel because he used to carry multiple passenger bags for the railroad around his neck and arms and he would even use a pole for leverage. For a dime a bag, he knew he could bring in a lot more money for the same amount of sweat and he didn't care how silly he looked.

Satchel has been documented as being the best and fastest pitcher of all times, and the oldest rookie to debut in Major League Baseball at 42 years of age.

When reporters questioned him in disbelief about how old he was, he would smile and say, "Age is a case of mind over matter. If you don't mind, it doesn't matter."

In 1948, when the branches of the armed forces were supposedly integrated according to Truman's Executive Order, Busby was hired as a Classification Specialist and his duties included handling military assignments, promotions, and transfers. After he retired, he worked as a benefits counselor for the Veterans Administration Regional Office. For six years, he was a city councilman for Teague, Texas, and the pro-tem mayor. In 1992, Mayor Bobby Wilkerson resigned after serving only two years of his term for a higher paying job. Ernest Busby filled the position and made history as the first Black mayor of Teague.

He wasn't interested in running for a full-term because he said he did not feel like raising somebody else's kids. And although the military placed him in elite positions because of his experience it did not eliminate his desire to pursue a bachelor's degree in business. He attended Tarlton State University, which was located in Stevensville, Texas, approximately 82 miles from his home. He said he didn't mind the drive, he did, however, mind not having a degree.

On his last day on earth, I was blessed to briefly talk with him. He mentioned the recent loss of his oldest daughter, Ernestine, and how he chose to stay in the car instead of attending her funeral because he didn't have the courage or the strength to place one foot in front of the other. He used to say that when he was feeling low he could always count on his day with Satchel Paige to give him a lift. Besides his wife and family, he said it was one of the fondest memories of his life.

- - - It is Written - - -

Five

★
PERIOD OF ADJUSTMENT

After three months on the Shaklee products, it was time for Veronica's follow up visit with her doctor. The diagnosis was not good. He advised her to become part of a case study that involved some of the top doctors in the country. She would have to undergo a surgical procedure that would require her to wear a colostomy bag for a limited amount of time. When she submitted to his wishes he had his assistants contact the other doctors to check their schedules. It was confirmed that the surgery would take place in two weeks.

In between working 12 hours at Sears, attending church on Sunday, and checking out as many library books as possible on cancer, I managed to save enough money to finally buy our first black and white television. The color television had made its way on the floors around this time-the late 1960s-but most of the shows I enjoyed watching were old westerns and classic movies which were in black and white, a habit I formed while in the Navy.

While at sea, we would have "Movie Matinee" night around 7:00 p.m. two to three times a week. A large projector screen was placed on the top deck and sometimes on the hanger deck, depending on the weather. When a western or classic was scheduled to be shown, I made sure I was seated in the front row.

I will never forget when the actors who starred in some of my favorite films like Gregory Peck, Edward G. Robinson, Burl Ives, and comedian Danny Kaye stopped by to give us words of encouragement. They wanted so much to lift our spirits and to let us know they were thankful that we had the courage to sacrifice our lives for the good of the country.

I didn't want to fill my days with worry because we all know what that invites in a hurry so I gave myself permission to enjoy a few shows. Watching television gave me the luxury of escaping from my unfortunate realities I was facing every day, and to be sure I didn't miss an episode I would set the alarm clock five minutes before it was scheduled to air.

During the operation, I knew Veronica was in the best hands in the world, but when I found out they were using Parke-Davis gold-plated surgical instruments, it eased my mind even more. When I got out of the Navy, I worked a few months at the Parke-Davis manufacturing plant polishing stainless steel medical products. One tray of the quality instruments would take hours to shine then I would place them on a shelf for inspection and from there they would go to a room to be plated in liquid gold.

The surgery was a success. Veronica woke up a little confused but more importantly all vitals were stable. When she came home, my job was to keep her sterile by emerging a solution through a tube into her rectum until it became completely closed. This was to stop the cancer from spreading.

Ronnie, the pet name I gave her, was healing wonderfully and feeling a lot better. We wanted to restart our lives, sort of pick up where we left off, so we began volunteering for Pastor Matthew Triplett at the

New Bethlehem Baptist Church. I was the Superintendent of Sunday School and Veronica was a member on the Stewardship Board and the Council of Changes. Her father was a minister so the conflicts, drama, and "what have yous" in the church was second nature to her. For me, it took some time getting used to. In less than a year, financial difficulties closed the doors of the church. Pastor Triplett decided to return to his former church, Mt. Zion in Redwood City, California, and a few months later, we joined St. James Methodist Church.

My son, Arby Jr., came to stay with us for the summer. He was 22 years old and it was the first time I saw him since he was around six years old. At first we were carrying on like strangers, not looking each other in the eyes, but when we started doing things together like going to the movies and working in the yard, past wounds began to gradually dissolve. Thank goodness I was faithful paying his momma Alma child support. I could only imagine the strain that would have caused let alone the embarrassment. For the first time, I had experienced what it felt like to have a family. Veronica loved that we were bonding-finally-and I was even open to making plans for the near future.

Arby Jr. left after a two month stay and said he would return soon. I missed him and I was surprised of how much. It was nice having him around and I thought the visit went well. Then I opened the phone bill and almost fell to the floor. The amount due was five times more than the basic monthly amount. I called him about it and he said that he was courting a young lady in Norfolk, Virginia, and that they had talked for hours. He apologized and promised to repay every cent. At that time, unlimited long distance was not an option. You were billed .25 to .50 cents a minute depending on the day and time you placed the call.

It was a lesson I needed to learn about parenting, which was the hardest job I ever attempted even though it was only for a short amount of time. I decided not to accept Arby Jr.'s money, but instead concentrate on what was more important in my life, something money could not replace, the health of my wife and the quality of time we had to spend together.

After months of back and forth discussions about moving to Teague, Texas, Ronnie convinced me that Momma Gussie's love and home cooked meals would definitely restore her health. She said her food was like medicine to the body and a healing to the soul. Before I could find a reason to oppose her idea, she had practically sold every item in our home. She even had the car serviced. All I could do was surrender.

The first month in Teague went smooth. Ronnie's energy increased and she spent more than a normal amount of time in Momma's garden planting vegetables. But then she began to feel faint and complained of sharp pains below the waist. We went to the town's doctor and he confessed that he was not familiar with this type of cancer or her procedure. He recommended an emergency appointment with her doctor. We packed a few things and hit the highway because we had every intention of returning to the place we began to call home.

This time, we sought the advice from a doctor in San Jose and once again the results of her exam were discouraging. The cancer returned but this time it was more aggressive. He did not want to remove the ovaries, but he had no other choice. After surgery, he placed his hand on my shoulder and said that with his deepest regrets the cancer had spread throughout her body and there was nothing more he could do. I shook his hand and thanked him.

I walked to my car, which was parked nearby, sat on "her" side and let the seat down as far as it would go. For the first time in my life, I allowed every emotion in my body to rear its face. I no longer wanted to act like I was a statue made of clay or a sidewalk made from cement. This wasn't the Navy, this was life and it was time for me to accept that losing a loved one comes with the territory.

I sobbed for not being able to grow old with

Ronnie, for the time my father left, the racial tensions I went through as a kid, the lack of necessities in our home, not finishing high school, for not being an attentive father, and for spending so much time in a military that never intended on promoting me pass the kitchen. I went on for a few hours, and as soon as the last tear drop fell on my drenched shirt, a light went off in my head and I began to see the silver linings in my life. I felt blessed for having a good wife, for loving a person's character and not caring about the color of their skin, for Momma and my son, and for being worthy enough to be assigned on the staff of great men. I thanked almighty God for these blessings up until the time I laid my head down on my pillow to rest.

When Ronnie came home, she would laugh then cry. After riding a week on this emotional rollercoaster, she finally found enough courage to update her family about the status of her health. At first they didn't believe her because she was always the little shop girl who could fight her way out of any situation no matter how impossible it seemed. They were confident her strength would defeat the cancer and one day soon she would call to say she was doing just fine. Her favorite cousin, Howard was optimistic and refused to accept that she was ill. He said, "Cousin Clara is a woman who could make cookies without the dough surely she could defeat this monster!"

Ronnie wanted to spend her last days in San Jose. She loved to fish so I rented an apartment near the ocean plus I thought the sound of the waves would ease some of her pain. Our insurance only covered the cost of a part-time nurse so I worked two jobs and filled in when she was off duty. Then Ronnie's condition worsened. She was re-admitted in O'Connor Hospital and two days later, while I was at home changing clothes to make my normal visit, I received a call that at 10:00 a.m. on the 21st of March in the year 1975, Ronnie's time on earth had expired.

For the last 10 years our lives together were the best. We took her illness and used it as a reminder to never waste time on regrets or missed opportunities and that every day above ground was a blessing. I promised her I would not complain but instead be forever grateful; it was a promise I planned to keep.

Most of her relatives lived in the Los Angeles area and I thought that since she loved them so much it would be wise to arrange for her final resting place to be there. It was a small and emotionally moving funeral without a lot of drawn out speeches. It was the way Veronica Clara "Ronnie" Pinkstonia would have wanted it to be.

A former shipmate and friend Leonard Starks called to offer his condolences. He said his wife Ruby became gravely ill and was admitted in a "home." He knew about my commitment to those who are shut-in and wondered if I could take a moment of my time to pay her a visit. "She would really enjoy seeing you," he said.

For the past five years, Ronnie and I volunteered at assistant care facilities. Every Monday, we would meet and greet patients. It hurt my heart to know that most of them had little or no family members who took time to check on them. Some didn't even have a change of clothes. I made it a special point to leave a piece of candy, a little stuffed animal, a pair of socks, or handwritten words of comfort on a card in their room. We often wondered if our last days would be spent there. Momma always said that you know where you been but you don't know where you're going.

As I walked through the doors at the convalescent care center, I braced myself for that distinct smell of life mixed with death coupled with medicine, cleaners, and urine to diminish from my nostrils. I normally placed Vicks VapoRub just above my upper lip, but since I was only going to visit one person I was sure I could tolerate the smell for that little amount of time.

I didn't recognize Sister Ruby. She was frail, totally opposite from the robust woman I was used to see coming a mile away. The last time I saw her she sang a solo in church so moving it left members searching for Kleenex and gasping for air. She opened her eyes and waved for me to come closer. I leaned down and she whispered, "It was me who caused the trouble between you and your wife and I am so sorry." I paused for a moment and repeated what I thought she said. She nodded and continued to recall certain incidents that alerted my memory of the times and places she was referring to. After the initial shock wore off, I forgave her, but deep down inside I hated her for being a back-stabbing so-called friend of ours. You never know the length of a snake until it is dead.

When I got home, Ruby's confession replayed in my head like a broken record. I started to remember vividly that one and only personal rough patch I had in my marriage. Ronnie was accusing me of wrong doings and I had no idea what her findings were based on. I had many sleepless nights and days on the couch, and for the life of me, I could not place my finger on where her feelings of doubt and anger were stemming from. I developed stomach ulcers and my appetite, what little I had, diminished. I replayed these dread awful moments in my head a few more times then I opened the living-room window and willed for them to leave and never come back. I was grateful she confessed because now I could finally put away the only puzzle I "owned" that had one piece missing. The next day, Leonard called and said Sister Ruby died peacefully in her sleep.

It was time to think about my life and where I should go from here. Living in San Jose brought back too many bad memories and I wasn't motivated when I was home in Teague; I simply existed. To make sure I was in touch with my feelings and these final thoughts were not just fragments of my imagination, I drove to Teague to see Momma and Charlie. I felt better but still it was only a resting place. Centerville was a 34 mile drive and while my heart was open to healing old wounds, I chose to take the drive alone.

It was nice to see old acquaintances and to learn

about the credible status of close friends. Mrs. Mary Langford, the woman who used to hit me on the side of my head when she caught me playing outside when the sun went down, looked well. She had just turned 89 years old and was looking forward to the big 9 0. I couldn't help but notice that leaning against the record player was an album by Sam "Lightnin'" Hopkins called "Texas Blues Man." She said she played it twice a day; in the morning and late at night.

Sam Hopkins was born in Centerville and his family was known to work all year on their little parcel of land, which explained why no one in the family and that included his four siblings could read or write. Ms. Mary remembered the day Sam's father, Abe, was killed while playing a card game called Pitty Pat. He tried to bluff a man named Floyd Johnson out of a buffalo nickel and he got mad and shot him. The family packed their things and moved to Leona, which is about seven miles south of Centerville.

I don't think anyone in the community was

surprised when Sam began to receive recognition around the world for the way he picked that guitar and sang those songs. When he was around four years old he would pick up anything on the ground or in the garbage that resembled a guitar and add a few strings. After working all day in the fields, and when he was not getting in some sort of trouble, he would sing the blues in front of a captive audience that included family members and kids in the neighborhood. He was born to live for music and in his later years he would add gambling, liquor, and women to that list.
In other words, he was just like his daddy Abe. Drinking was something they did to please their mind.

On January 30, 1982, Sam Lightnin' Hopkins died from esophageal cancer. He was buried in Houston, Texas, where he resided, and in 2002 the town of Crockett, Texas, dedicated a 500 pound statue in "Lightnin' Hopkins Park" in his memory. I never met anyone who could cock a fedora hat and wear dark Ray Ban sunglasses like Sam. He wore shades all the time and when asked why he said, "I'm a hidin' man. I been hidin' all my life."

I was becoming restless and tired of the daily reminders of the way things were. I was ready to make a bold move. Uncle O.C. and Aunt Georgia lived in Las Vegas for 10 years and they had been trying to convince me to relocate there because they thought the hot temperature during the summer would benefit Ronnie's health. She loved playing the one-arm bandits and at one time gave it some serious thought but her illness only allowed for small changes not large ones.

Cheetah was 12 years old and one morning she started showing signs of fatigue. She stopped eating and was having a difficult time standing up for more than a few seconds. The vet said it was time to put her down and after considerable thought I agreed. The next day, I drove to the animal clinic and parked the car and could not for the life of me open the door. I looked at Cheetah and she looked at me. She still had a little life in her and I didn't have the courage to end it.

The only person from my hometown, Centerville, Texas, who made a name for himself was legend guitarist, songwriter, and country blues singer, Sam "Lightnin'" Hopkins. He was one of the greatest influences on rock guitar players.

My wife Veronica brought a lot of joy to my life. She was my soul-mate and the dog Cheetah was her heart. I was devastated when I learned her cancer returned.

After two more failed attempts, it was time to make a realistic decision. As I gently sat her on the table, I held her paw until her eyes closed. It was time for me to say goodbye to the last direct link to the fondest memories of my life.

I donated everything in the apartment to charity, and placed only the daily necessities in my 1969, 88-Royal Oldsmobile. I was entering the valley of the shadow of doubt, and I would fear no evil. And what better time to make my move than in March of 1976.

- - - It is Written - - -

Six

★
THEM BRIGHT LIGHTS

When I arrived in Las Vegas, I felt like I was this country boy from a little town in Texas who had the nerves to live in a place millions of tourists visited on a weekly basis. Instead of renting a room or an apartment, I lived with Uncle O.C. and Aunt Georgia. They were church goers who also had a fondness for gambling.

The freedom to go out any hour of the night to play keno or the machines was appreciated. I found myself hanging out with them at their favorite joints. During the day, while they were at work, I started to frequent "their" spots more than I would ever dare to admit. I grew afraid of being seen by a family acquaintance so I decided to visit Ernie's Bar, which was located less than four miles from where I was living. I was told one of the bus depot's for Nevada Test Site workers was located a few blocks away and they would often stop by after work, and quite a number of them served in the military. I must admit, nothing would please me more than to bump into an old shipmate to swap stories, compare our military experiences, and to find out who traveled the furthest.

Ernie's was small and quaint. I immediately found a machine in a dark corner and signaled for the Change Girl. A slot machine mechanic started repairing the one-armed bandit next to me and I noticed a large eagle was tattooed on his forearm, a clear indication he served in the military. I introduced myself and asked about his years in the "hole." He laughed.

His name was Erwin Wilburn and he was drafted in the Army in 1944 and was enlisted with the Company 'B' 1332 Engineer Regiment in Camp Ellis, Illinois, an all Black unit. Camp Ellis was not only for training it was a concentration camp for German prisoners of war.

My return visits to Ernie's Bar to play my favorite keno machine widened and the discussions with Erwin about our times in service deepened. He mentioned that he had an Army buddy named George Kirby and he later became a worldly actor-comedian.

Back row-left, second: In July 1944, Erwin Wilburn was drafted by the Army and enlisted with Company 'B' 1332 Engineer Regiment in Camp Ellis, Illinois. Standing to his right is friend George Kirby who later became a famous actor-comedian.

After Sergeant Erwin "Brother" Wilburn was discharged, he became the first Black slot machine mechanic in Las Vegas.

I asked around about George and discovered that he lived in Las Vegas and at one time produced his own television show. He was a master at imitating someone or something and was one of the first premiere Black actors who appealed to a White audience in the mid-60s. Unfortunately, he became an occasional drug user which led to selling them. In 1977, he was caught and sentenced to a 10 year prison term but only had to serve 42 months.

It was time to disconnect from the comfort of military talks and admit I had developed a gambling habit and if I didn't make a quick change, my biggest fear of amounting to nothing would soon manifest.

You are only as good as the company you keep and when you lie down with dogs you wake up with fleas. I couldn't ignore these truths. I packed my belongings and moved into a small, quaint house that was located in the same community, which is often referred to as the "Historic Westside." It was the designated area Blacks were forced to live in during segregation. Jim Crow made a pit stop in Las Vegas as well.

Las Vegas may be known as the "Entertainment Capitol of the World", but the Westside was known as the "Church Capitol." There are close to 130 churches located within an eight mile radius. In other words, you could be kicked out the back door of one church and walk right into the front door of another.

My first order of business was to be an active member in a Baptist church, but I needed to make a few more visits before I made that commitment. Since most of the sermons sounded better than the last one, I church hopped for two years. During service, I would write down the scriptures mentioned in the preacher's message to make sure the meanings were accurate, a habit I started in 1960 when I was 34 years old.

When I was stationed in San Diego, I attended a Baptist church. The preacher sounded so eloquent reciting scriptures from memory. After service, I sat in a coffee shop and wrote down every scripture that was mentioned. When I got back on the ship, I researched their meanings according to a King James Version of the Bible. I couldn't believe what I found. The preacher's definition was nowhere near God's interpretation. He misquoted and misinterpreted every one of them. They call that "puppeteering from the pulpit." Today, during sermons, I will jot down brief notes to make sure their meanings were used accurately. I carry extra pens and paper in case someone left home without them. I think it's a sin for an individual to miss an opportunity to capture knowledge they can literally take home with them.

In 1978, I narrowed my search for a "church home" down to one. I chose Second Baptist Church because it was located on 500 Madison Avenue, and a few blocks from Jackson Street, our "Black Strip", which were both within walking distance from where I lived. Everything I needed was at the tip of my fingers and there was enough going on in the area to keep my mind busy and off the pain that was starting to subside but yet continued to linger. I enjoyed the sermons from the newly appointed pastor, Reverend Willie Davis, and I found the history of the church quite entertaining.

Second Baptist was founded on February 22, 1942, and the first pastor was Reverend B.T. Mayfield. The parcel of land was donated by one of its members, Mary Nettles, and the contributions from the congregation helped build the church. Reverend Mayfield was a great speaker but due to his indiscretions he only served six months as the pastor.

After service, the church janitor, Johnny Johnson, would walk around to make sure no one was in the building. Once the coast was clear, he would start to sweep the front entrance. On this particular evening, he overheard two people laughing in a lowered voice. It was faint but as he walked closer it was obvious he wasn't alone. His mouth opened as he stood and watched Reverend B.T. Mayfield and a woman lying naked on top of the collection table. Just to make sure it was Pastor Mayfield we walked a little closer and

Second Baptist Church was founded in 1942. Front-center holding Bible is Reverend B.T. Mayfield the first pastor. He was a good speaker but unfortunately his indiscretions cost him his position.

The sixth pastor, Reverend Willie Davis, preceded Reverend Joseph Jefferson in 1978, the year I joined.

adjusted his glasses. As soon as the initial shock wore off, he rushed out the door and crossed the street to the house where one of the members on the Mother Board lived. Sweat poured from Johnny's forehead as he described every detail which included birthmarks, moles, and childhood scars.

The next day, an emergency meeting with just the Mother Board was held at the church. A unanimous vote was taken to remove B.T. from his position. Eugene "Peve" Buford, the grandson of Mary Nettles and the only man I have ever known to be thrown out of a choir simply because he couldn't sing, summarized the hot steamy scene better than anyone. He said, "B.T. was caught putting tail feathers in an angel."

Reverend Mayfield relocated to Reno, Nevada and the whereabouts of his female companion were unknown. Private First Class Buford served in the Army during the Korean War and Johnny Johnson joined the military around the same time I was drafted. He enlisted with the Army, Navy, and Air Force, and served during three war eras-WWII, Korean, and Vietnam.

My activities at Second Baptist became extensive and rewarding. I joined the Brotherhood program and our mission was to support the pastor and outreach to the community. The members were so inspired by my ideas and the ability to follow through on commitments I was voted president-a position I held for 27 years.

My first order of business was to not allow the homeless to walk off the streets and into the fellowship hall. This posed a danger to the church and to the members because they were known to take anything they could and sale for drugs. It was hard to know who was telling the truth and who was lying. I took a chance and decided to help a man named Gus.

Gus was confident he could clean up his act and get off drugs if he was staying with his family in the Los Angeles area. He asked me for money to buy a bus ticket but I took the initiative and purchased it. The next morning, about 1:00 a.m., an agent at the station called and said Gus tried to cash in his ticket and to come down and pick up my refund. I could only hope Gus was the last of the program's issue, but boy was I wrong.

The Brotherhood meeting took place every Tuesday at 7:00 p.m. After devotion, I was informed that Deacon Ranzo Webb had been kidnapped. His wife told one of the members that he had called to say he would be home the next day, but when that didn't happen she filed a missing persons report with the Las Vegas Metropolitan Police Department.

Some of the church leaders and most of the members did not panic about his disappearance. They were quite aware of his fondness of other women, and when they heard his bank accounts were emptied, they were confident a pretty little angel was somewhere in the picture. Even so, there were still quite a few who believed he really was kidnapped and being held hostage somewhere.

The story told to me was that one night while

Deacon Webb, an armed security guard, was on post at a commercial building located on Harmon Avenue, two White men shoved a gun in his face and demanded he drive his 1988, Dodge Ramcharger to a specified section of town to pick up a friend. They forced him to fill the gas tank and then drove to San Diego, California, which was approximately 362 miles. When they arrived within city limits, they looked for the nearest Wells Fargo bank. He walked inside with two of the men on each side and withdrew all of the funds from his checking and savings account. When the kidnappers returned to the car, to be less conspicuous, they drove down surface streets when suddenly the car broke down. The three men fled, and Deacon Webb ran to the nearest phone booth to call the police. Within a month, the two men who were escaped convicts were captured.

At the trial, Deacon Webb's testimony placed the kidnappers behind bars for a long-time. It took two years for me to find the perfect time and place to ask Deacon Webb about the day he was missing.

The 2007 Second Baptist Church Ministers and Deacon Board. Deacon Ranzo Webb (front-middle) wearing dark sunglasses, was kidnapped and held hostage for one week. The late Deacon James Robinson (right-back row, second) was the longest standing living member at Second Baptist. He joined in 1946.

The Usher Board sponsored a bus for the members of the Brotherhood to attend the funeral of a long-time member, Brother Berry, in Phoenix, Arizona. I was seated next to Deacon Webb, and he repeated the same story I was told. Even today, at 88 years old, he still says that he was missing for a week because he was held hostage at gunpoint. Regardless of what is continued to be said some 30 years later that contradicts his story, I have decided to stick with my good and faithful friend's version of what he considered to be the truth and nothing but, even though I have yet to meet one person who had attended the trial.

The Second Baptist Choir had won some of the most prestigious competitions on the west coast. They had emerged from being a group of locals to becoming highly acclaimed. A few of us members in the Brotherhood program thought about initiating a male chorus, but first I needed to run it by Reverend Willie Davis. He thought the idea had potential and there were enough male singers to give it legs. I asked the

President of the Usher Board, Deacon Willis Warren, to assist us, and he was more than willing. Reverend Eddie Shields volunteered, but he became more of a mentor and friend than an advisor.

For over 10 years, Reverend Shields was a detective for the Las Vegas Metropolitan Police Department. Whenever he got the chance, he loved telling the story about the time he and his White partner transported a White criminal on a Greyhound bus.

Detective Shields and his partner obtained custody of a criminal in a small town in Southern California. When they boarded a passenger bus at the station, he sat across from them. After traveling a few miles, Shields unbuttoned his jacket and accidently exposed his holster that contained a concealed weapon. A White woman walked by and when she saw the gun she screamed, "Hey look, there is a Black man on the bus with a gun!" The bus driver, who was well aware of what the detectives were doing, just shook his head and ignored her.

During Sunday service, one of the deacons announced that the church was starting a male chorus program and urged all men with singing potential to join. The response was overwhelming. A program was launched, and in 1987, the Second Baptist Male Chorus was founded.

Rehearsal was three times a week and Cecil Davis, the choir leader and organizer, said that a debut was not going to happen until we reached that sweet choral sound and that hitting a high note does not necessarily contribute to the overall goal. We finally sounded like we were on one accord; it was time for us to be heard and not just seen.

After four years of singing and swaying back and forth in churches and at conventions, our 40 member male chorus was recognized as the most "Outstanding Male Chorus of Southern Nevada." It would not have happened, however, if Cecil did not remain razor focused, a skill he credits the United States Air Force where he served 26 years and retired as a Major, for

Second Baptist Church Male Chorus. I am standing, left, front. It was February, Black History Month, and we had just won a competition. Standing (front,-middle) is Cecil Davis the choir leader and organizer. He would later become labeled the "whistle blower" during the Reverend Davis federal trial.

sharpening.

In the Navy, I became known for my mouth-watering Texas style brisket. I wanted to prepare the dish for an upcoming church picnic but was unsuccessful finding a store who sold the meat and a resident who even heard of it. My brother-in-law, Ernest Busby, sent a few boxes from Mexia, Texas, to the Nellis Air Force Base Commissary. Military personnel who are active and retired have limited access to the use of the store, and unlimited travel on a plane if space is available.

At the picnic, those who wanted to just sample the meat were satisfied and curious. "What is this?" they asked. Now I am not saying I brought brisket to Las Vegas, I am simply indicating that at the time I had not met anyone who experienced eating the slow cooked, perfectly sliced meat. My brisket was so tender you didn't "need no teef to eat my beef."

I filled the majority of my days with church activities. I was living a purpose filled life where there was no reminder of the past then father time started meddling with my conscience. I remembered that it's been a while since I seen Momma Gussie. Grandma Lorraine, God rest her soul, used to say talking over the phone was no substitute for sitting with someone, no matter how convenient it was.

A few days later, I was in the car and on my way to Teague. I stopped in Phoenix, Arizona, to visit my former shipmate, Lieutenant Commander Hollingsworth, and I took the advice from my Aunt Maggie and visited my biological father, Sam Hambric, Jr. She was keeping me up to date on his overall health and well-being both the good and the bad so I knew he would welcome me with open arms.

It was the first time I had seen him since the day he turned that piece of steel we called a door handle and walked out without saying goodbye. He looked a little frail and I saw a little resemblance. Our conversations weren't hurried or strained, and I didn't ask him why he left because I was raised to never question grown folks. I wanted to go forward and be at peace with the bond we were trying to establish. After four days and three nights, I hit the highway and headed for Teague, Texas. I felt good about taking that first step towards getting to know the man who was legally considered my "real" father.

My mother Gussie and step-dad Charlie were in good health. I didn't care what I did when I went home just as long as it included quiet moments and honest talks with Momma on the front porch. Our "sessions" always seemed to warm my soul and restore my faith leaving me breathless without a stain and capable of handling difficulties with a smile.

A few years later, Aunt Maggie said that Sam became gravely ill and she arranged for him to live with her in Denver, Colorado. She thought it would be wise for me to be by his side when he took his last breath, but on the day I planned to leave she called and said it was too late. The man I heard much about but knew very little was gone. I didn't feel any guilt so therefore there was no reason to grieve. I was simply grateful I took the time to spend with him when he was of sound mind and body.

One year later, the only man I considered to be my father, Charlie Levels, was having heart complications. On Christmas day, about six in the morning, he decided to call every family member instead of waiting on the usual calls from us which was normally around noon. He was determined to speak to each of us and not to a darn answering machine. After he made the last call, Momma said he sighed with relief, placed the received down, and slumped over in the chair. When the paramedics arrived, they checked his vitals. He was pronounced dead.

Momma and Charlie made good with what they were given. They prayed together, laughed and spoke to each other with all due respect. He treated us as if we were his own. He had four children with his first wife, but the only time I spent with them was in the cotton fields and at school.

On November 21, 2005, three days shy of my 79th birthday, would be my own personal day of destruction. My sister Mildred called and said Momma Gussie died in her sleep at a convalescent home. She was 98 years old. I felt faint and my hands weakened, but somehow I held on to the phone. I had a schoolmate visiting at the time so I used every bit of my strength to hold myself together; I didn't want her to feel sad while she was on vacation. But when she left, for the second time in my life, my emotions got the best of me. It felt like a grenade exploded inside my chest. I made a safe landing and waved a flag of surrender. I prayed for gratitude because I knew I was blessed for having a momma to enjoy throughout my entire youth and the majority of my adult years. I was there when she needed me and knowing this gave me perfect peace. I just wish I would have told her more often how proud I was of her.

In 1986, at the age of 79 years old, Momma completed her G.E.D. Her cousin, Lacey Watts, taught

Momma Gussie celebrating her 90th birthday. Next to me is my sister Rosa Lee, and Mildred with her husband, Ernest Busby, the first Black Mayor of Teague, Texas.

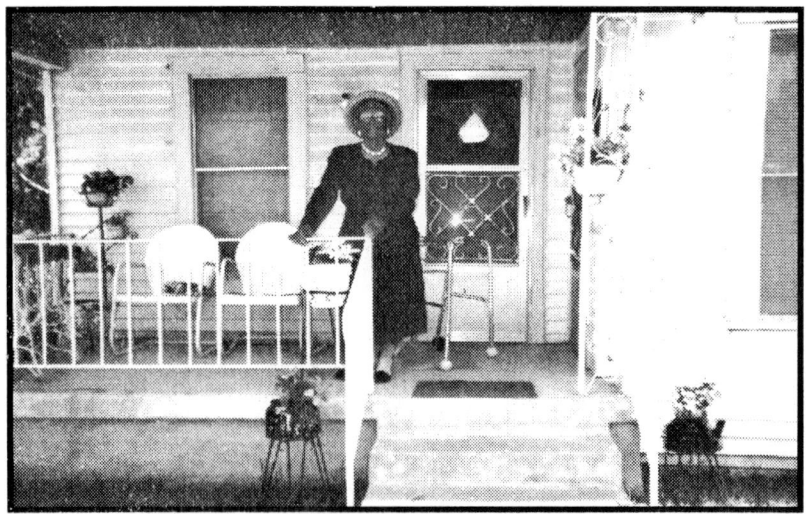

Lots of wisdom was shared on Momma Gussie's front porch. Her "sessions" were collard greens for my soul.

relocated back to Teague, Texas, and initiated a program for those interested in getting a G.E.D. at Momma's second home, a nearby senior center. She only went as far as the sixth grade so she assumed it would take "forever" to complete the required classes, but instead it took two full years. Momma said the first time she saw her name printed in "those fancy raised letters" on her diploma she felt worthy and accepted.

Having to say goodbye to those dearest to my heart created an alarming need to get acquainted with my remaining family members especially our future generations. I thought about the loose ends in my life, those I had yet to meet and get to know, and that meant more than just their names. I wondered if I said everything there was to say to Arby Jr. or was there more and if so what? He talked a lot about his two daughters, Vicki and Dyshell, and his most precious jewels, Vicki's son, Lil' Roland; and Dyshell's daughter, Dekeara, and son, Taquan.

The majority of the family was located in Norfolk,

Virginia. Every year, around June when the kids were out of school for the summer, I flew down and stayed at the Norfolk Naval Base in the Transit Quarters. I arranged for Arby Jr. to have coffee with me a few times but he never showed nor did he provide any kind of explanation when I saw him at one of the family functions. I wasn't ready to presume that he was not interested in developing a close bond, not yet, but the wheels were definitely turning in that direction.

Dyshell, Arby Jr.'s youngest daughter, stayed in contact with just about everyone in the family. Periodically, I called to find out the latest headlines, and to remind her to keep me posted on which of the 23 college football scholarships her son, Taquan, ends up selecting. When she told me he chose the University of Virginia in Charlottesville, which was 178 miles from their home in Virginia Beach, I was elated he wanted to attend such an accredited school and more importantly to be near his family.

I was impressed with Taquan, the young man,

From left, my granddaughters, Vicki and Dyshell, who was pregnant with Taquan at the time. After Momma died, I made annual visits to Norfolk to get acquainted with the family I never knew.

Left: Brandon, my granddaughter Vicki's husband, her son Lil' Roland, and Arby Jr. It was fulfilling spending time with my great-grandson who I discovered had a whole lot on his mind.

In 2013, I was bubbling with pride when I watched my great-grandson, Taquan "Smoke" Mizzell playing on national television in the "All-American High School Bowl" even though it was for the U.S. Army.

Signing Day. Out of the 23 collegiate schools, Taquan chose the University of Virginia to be close to home. From right, front: Grandma Dot (Dorothy Hambric) his mom, Dyshell, and sister Dekeara. Left-back: Cousin Jerome Williams and Dyshell's boyfriend Courtney Littlejohn.

the moment I met him. His dad was absent from his life, in and out of jail most of his life, but he was fortunate that Dyshell's husband at that time, Kamal Gardner, wanted to play a major role during his developmental years, a hat not all step-dads are willing and able to wear.

I remember like it was yesterday sitting on the porch shelling peas, cleaning collards, shucking corn when Momma said, "You know a conversation could change a person's life." Then she added, "Believe it or not, there are some good White folks out there."

My long-time friend, Mother Patterson, introduced me to Colonel Floyd "Buckshot" White. She had been the family's maid for over 20 years and she believed all military men should know each other so they could share war stories. Colonel White served 30 years (1940-1970) in the Air Force and earned the nickname "Buckshot" because of his ability to make quick decisions while in the midst of battle.

In addition to his military background, he was

the founder of a prison ministry and a devout Episcopalian, but he didn't endorse a particular religion, he simply taught the word of God from a King James Version of the Bible.

My first mission with Colonel White was to the High Desert State Prison in Indian Springs, Nevada. We drove approximately 45 minutes before arriving at the entrance gate. As we traveled towards the front, I couldn't help but stare at the razor barbed wire fence that framed the complex. Then when the Colonel reiterated there were 800 plus inmates behind those walls my mind started playing tricks on me. I imagined tomorrow's newspaper headlines as being, "Prison Outbreak At High Desert-Hostages Taken." I never visited anyone in prison and nor have I spent one day in one. I got scarred and had no idea what to expect but I decided to bend instead of break. As we entered the prison, I stood tall and walked with conviction like the soldier I was taught to be.

I assumed the inmates enjoyed the Colonel

Colonel Floyd "Buckshot" White was one of the most decorated pilots in the United States Air Force. After serving 30 years, he retired and started a prison ministry that I briefly became part of. In 1995, Nellis Air Force Base named a building "White Hall" in his honor.

because he was such a nice man, and he cared deeply, but when he walked in the chapel, the men stood and gave the most sincere slanted salute I was blessed to witness. It was eye-opening to be in the presence of inmates from different races who were so heavily engrossed in reading God's word. After the "lesson plan of the day" was finished, they insisted Colonel White tell one of his stories about his life and times in the Air e morning when we were scheduled to make another visit, his wife Fran called and said that the Colonel was feeling a little under the weather and asked if I would fill in for him on "National Prayer Day", which was the first Thursday of May. I accepted.

I stood on the steps of the Las Vegas City Hall with other missionaries praying for peace and unity in our country. The next day, May 6, 1994, Colonel Floyd "Buckshot" White went to be with the Lord.

In 1995, Nellis Air Force Base in Las Vegas, Nevada, honored Colonel White by dedicating a building in his honor, White Hall. Judging from the people who attended the event, he didn't just associate with officers in the Air Force, he hung out with military personnel from every division and folks from all walks of life.

I admired Colonel White's bravery and the endless time he gave to those who found themselves in helpless positions. He was a humanitarian and the most delightful person, besides Momma Gussie and Charlie, I have ever been around. It was an honor to have "served" with such a man of God.

- - - It is Written - - -

Seven

---★---
THE WORTH
OF IT ALL

On April 12, 1981, the breaking news across the globe and the topic of conversations in practically every social gathering was that former heavyweight champion boxer, Joseph Louis Barrow died from cardiac arrest. He was 66 years old. Muhammad Ali said, "From Black folks to redneck Mississippi crackers, they loved him. They're all crying. That shows you. Howard Hughes dies, with all his billions, not a tear. Joe Louis, everybody cried." Joe and his wife Martha lived comfortably in a home that was once owned by NBC talk show host and comedian, Johnny Carson. They were long-time residents of Las Vegas.

Although the latter years of his life was plagued by the IRS, drugs, a stroke, and bouts of paranoia, at least the last event he attended, according to a reliable source, was "one of the best boxing matches he had ever seen." In a 15-round unanimous decision, heavyweight champion Larry Holmes defended his title when he defeated Trevor Berbick. Joe sat ringside at the Pavilion in a wheelchair that read on the back "Property of

Caesars Palace."

An announcement requesting volunteers to usher at Joe Louis' memorial was made at Second Baptist Church. I felt obligated. Joe's story was a past importance to my life, an ending with a new beginning, and a promise without cost.

The services took place at the Caesars Palace Sports Pavilion. For the viewing, his widow, Martha Jefferson Louis, insisted his body be placed on a platform in the shape of a boxing ring. She said, "Joe's life was in the ring. He would have wanted it this way. It seems appropriate." However, many felt her idea was everything but that, but Martha could care less about the opinion of others.

Civil rights activist, Reverend Jesse Jackson, delivered a touching eulogy in front of 3,000 people who came to say goodbye to their champ. I was assigned to the section that was reserved for the family. There were no emotional outbursts, just a few tears.

The burial was initially scheduled to be held at

Palm Mortuary in Las Vegas, but that was unacceptable to Martha. She made calls to powerful political friends and demanded, with a sweet demeanor, they get in touch with President Ronald Reagan as soon as possible. When Reagan's office called, she emphasized that Joe served in the Army and was considered an American hero, and therefore the proper burial site for his final resting place should be the Arlington National Cemetery. President Reagan agreed. He waived the burial eligibility rules for her dearly beloved, and on April 21, 1981, surrounded by 800 friends and family members, Joe Louis was buried among military icons such as: former President John F. Kennedy – a Lieutenant in the Navy; Civil Rights Leader, Medgar Evers – a Sergeant in the Army; Four-Star Army General Benjamin O. Davis, Sr.; and Four-Star Air Force General Daniel Chappie James, Jr. Max Schmeling who was once an opponent and later a good friend was one of the pallbearers.

Martha met Joe in 1958, when she handled his

short-lived divorce from his second wife, Rose Morgan, a beauty salon tycoon. She was known as the "attorney to the stars", and notably recognized as being one of the first Black female lawyers to be licensed in the State of California, and the first Black to lease an office on Wilshire Boulevard in Beverly Hills. She was once married to Bernard S. Jefferson, a California appellate judge, legal scholar, and the first Black to be appointed to the state appellate courts.

Martha was a petite fearless woman whose distinct look included wearing glasses on top of her head and walking with a slight limp that developed in her later years. When it came to rescuing Joe, she pushed her disability aside to help him escape from scandals that could have gone viral. She also willingly adopted the children he fathered outside their marriage.

Approximately seven years after Joe's death, Martha's diabetes worsened and insulin injections were required. When Rose Morgan, Joe's second wife, found out she was in poor health, she flew Martha to her

In 1955, Joe Louis married second wife, beauty salon tycoon, Rose Morgan.

In March 1959, Joe Louis marriage third wife, attorney Martha Jefferson. She handled his divorce from second wife, Rose.

home in Detroit and arranged full-time nursing care. The medical attention, fundraising dinners, and elite crowd may have extended her life, but they did little to restore her overall health. On August 2, 1991, at the age of 79, Martha Jefferson Louis died in a convalescent home and was buried alongside her beloved Joe-in the Arlington National Cemetery.

Before I enlisted in the Navy, Joe Louis volunteered to join the Army in 1942. It was during the WWII era and the government wanted the general public to buy bonds to help pay for the war. Joe's contributions to the Army was marketing this concept and fighting in charitable boxing matches. But even though it was a sincere gesture, the I.R.S. demanded he pay his fair share from the winnings he earned before and during his years in the Army. This marked the beginning of his financial woes.

I would have fallen overboard if Joe Louis would have been assigned to one of the ships I was on. Instead, professional boxers, Floyd Patterson and Sugar

Ray Robinson, came on board to host exhibition fights, which included the sailors who had grave interests in boxing. A stage was built for this special occasion.

Joe was a fighter in and out of the ring. He spoke up for Black soldiers and helped officers gain entrance in the Officer Candidate School at Fort Riley, Kansas. One of those applicants was a young, eager soldier named Jackie Robinson and he would later break Major League Baseball's color barrier.

On April 15, 1947, Jackie made his debut as a Brooklyn Dodger and became the first Black to play in the league. He was also a track and football scholar at U.C.L.A. (University of California, Los Angeles) and a civil rights activist for Black players.

Martha used to say that if anyone wanted to find Joe all they had to do was walk around Caesars Palace's casino or check the nearest golf course. His passion for golf was almost as strong as it was for boxing. In fact, it was rumored that the reason he was knocked out in the

Joe having a laugh with privates on the base. In 1942, he volunteered to join the U.S. Army. His charitable boxing matches raised a substantial amount for the Army but concerns with the I.R.S.

first match against Max Schmeling was because he was in the gym. Joe loved to bet even though his game was considered decent. Lots of "Benjamin Franklins" passed through those hands that were once known for landing the fastest and most powerful punches in the history of boxing.

Joe got tired of being an "easy target" on the golf course so he hired Ted Rhodes, one of America's first skilled Black golfers, to help elevate his game. He became his personal instructor and playing partner and seldom did they lose. Theodore "Ted" Rhodes was a friend of my longtime shipmate, Robert Skates. Ted served in the Navy during World War II and when it ended, in 1945 his discharge landed him in Chicago, Illinois. He became a close associate of Joe who introduced him to his wife, Claudia, a dancer known to have the fastest feet in the entertainment industry. They had two daughters, Peggy and Deborah.

Ted Rhodes won over 150 tournaments and the majority of them were played on segregated golf

From left: Leonard Reid, Bill Spiller, Ted Rhodes, and Joe Louis warming up to play on a segregated golf course.

Former Army veteran legendary golf pro, Theodore "Ted" Rhodes taught Joe Louis the fundamentals of golf. When Tiger Woods won his first Masters Tournament, he acknowledged Ted for making the opportunity possible for him.

courses and hosted by the United States Colored Golfers now called the United Golfers Association. George Adams founded U.G.A. because golf was considered a White man's sport and Coloreds were not allowed to play, only caddie. The prize money was meager which made it virtually impossible for a player to support his family. No matter how many tournaments Ted and his partner, Bill Spiller, won by huge margins the Professional Golfers Association of America (P.G.A.) continued to reject their application. Ted was a stylish, quiet man with an effortless swing who let his golf clubs do the talking. His partner, Billy Spiller, was highly educated and not afraid to speak against discrimination. When his application was rejected, he demanded an explanation.

The P.G.A. told him that due to their "Caucasian only" clause, they could not allow Coloreds. Ted, Bill, and Madison Gunther, also a Black pro golfer, filed a lawsuit against them, but before it went to court an agreement was reached. It was decided that Coloreds could play in the P.G.A. only if they were invited by a sponsor. The word tournament was replaced with invitational, which gave the P.G.A. even more jurisdiction to allow whomever they wanted to play in their tournaments.

In 1950, the Joe Louis 'The Champ' Golf Course was opened in Riverdale, Illinois, and in 1963, Joe became the first Black invited to play with a sponsored exemption in the P.G.A.'s San Diego Open. Things were changing but not fast enough.

When Ted Rhodes returned home to his roots in Nashville, Tennessee, he mentored professional notable golfers like Lee Elder and Charlie Sifford. On July 4, 1969, at 55 years of age, he died. He was inducted into the Nashville Hall of Fame for golfers, and in his memory, the City of Nashville renamed the Cumberland Golf Course the Ted Rhodes Golf Course.

In 2009, the P.G.A. granted honorary memberships to Ted Rhodes, Bill Spiller, John Shippen, and Joe Louis. I was sad just knowing none of them

In 2009, at the Annual Meeting in New Orleans, (left) Hanno Shippen-Smith, Deborah Rhodes, and Billy Spiller, Jr. accepted P.G.A. honorary memberships on behalf of their fathers who paved the way for Black golfers today. Joe Louis was also a recipient.

were alive to witness how much their courageous efforts paid off. In April 1997, when professional champion golfer, Tiger Woods won his first Masters Tournament, he acknowledged Lee Elder, Charlie Sifford, and Ted Rhodes. He said, "I am the first minority to win here, but I wasn't the first to play. That was Lee Elder, and my hats off to him and Charlie Sifford and Ted Rhodes who made this possible for me."

- - - It is Written - - -

Eight

★
MIRACLE ON MADISON AVENUE

It was entertainer Frank Sinatra, Jr. who said, "Las Vegas is the exit off the freeway to Sodom and Gomorrah." I can honestly say that after living in the city since 1978, there is definitely some validity to his words.

On March 17, 1991, the congregation at Second Baptist celebrated the grand opening of the church's Phase 1 expansion plan. Reverend Jesse Jackson, who was paid $10,000 to attend the event, according to Reverend Davis who boasted about it, honored the church and gave her the title, "Miracle on Madison Avenue."

Throughout the years, I developed a close relationship with the leader of Second Baptist Church, Reverend Willie Davis. I thought of him as an upright family man and a strong leader in the community. When his wife Jeanette was diagnosed with cancer, he became disoriented. A friend of the family, Reverend Willie Jacobs, felt they could use some moral support so he introduced them to his cousin, Emma, a woman of the church who provided spiritual comfort to grieving families. She lived in Detroit but was known to visit relatives quite often in the Las Vegas area.

The congregation was stricken with grief when they learned Jeanette lost her battle to cancer, and to our surprise, Reverend Davis handled her death better than we had expected. We began to take notice how often Emma was in town and how frequent he was missing from the pulpit. His explanation was that his mother, who also resided in Detroit, was very ill and he wanted to be there for her. Then news swirled in the church like a dust storm in the desert that Reverend Davis and Emma were married in a private ceremony in Detroit.

Most of us saw the writing on the wall. However, one of the women he was courting was very upset about the news. She demanded that Davis return the expensive cowboy boots and tailor-made business suits she bought and repay the money he supposedly borrowed.

Shortly after they tied the knot, signs of an

implosion began to occur within the church. In 2002, when a $423,000 department of justice grant was awarded to develop a transitional housing program and facility for pre-release prisoners, the members suspected that the Davis' were doing everything with the money but what was promised. There were no simply signs that the construction for the program's housing was underway. And when their list of personal material possessions suddenly increased, those daunting questions on most of our minds ceased to exist.

They had purchased a new Mercedes sedan and a slightly used Rolls-Royce from a private owner in Alabama. I must admit, Reverend Davis was the first person I've known to have the guts to travel to the deep-south with unguarded money. He said, "I took a briefcase full of church money and a gun tucked between a stack of Benjamin." He was born in Boligee, a little town in the county of Tuscaloosa, Alabama. In 2000, the population was 368 and 80% were Black and I am willing to bet that those stats were similar to the ones recorded when he was a little boy.

In 1978, Reverend Davis and his first wife Jeanette along with their two children relocated to Las Vegas from Utah. On the day they arrived, their station-wagon broke down. Jewell Scott, the Chairman of the Deacon Board, donated his 1956 white, Cadillac sedan to the family. He said, "Ole Rev drove that car until the wheels came off!"

My fondness for Reverend Davis' began when I learned that he made time in his busy schedule to escort and give the eulogy at veteran funerals in Boulder City, Nevada, which was about 34 miles from Las Vegas. I informed him that every since 1956, I had been a traveling flag bearer for all branches of the United States Military, and that the lives of veterans are lost every minute of the day and they deserve to be buried with dignity and honor. He both agreed that to have no one available to hand the 13-folded flag to the family would be a disgrace to this country. The American flag is a symbol of strength and unity and it is either draped or folded at every veteran funeral. We consider the flowers to be inside the casket-that being the body of the veteran.

Then one day, he told me that driving to Boulder City just to conduct a committal service at a veteran's funeral was a waste of gas. He felt that the amount he was paid for his services did not cover the traveling expense. I almost lost my mind. I told him he was unpatriotic and I will be there for the families no matter what. He stared at me and I stared back at him and neither one of us owed each other money.

I felt divided and stuck and I did not want to suspect anything illegal was going on with the Davis'. I presumed that since they religiously drove to the Nevada state line to play the California Lottery that maybe one of them hit the Megabucks, but when the F.B.I. started investigating their records I knew that was definitely not the case. According to the <u>Las Vegas Sun</u> newspaper, Ms. Emma went into a local bank to sign documents for a $90,000 loan and mistakenly used a social security number that was different from the one she had previously used. The bank representative noticed it and immediately reported it to the F.B.I.

When the feds were searching in Ms. Emma's backyard, they accidentally bumped into Cecil along the way. Cecil Davis, no relation to Willie, was my friend and the Male Chorus leader. He worked for the sister company the pre-release program was structured under called the Alliance Collegiums Association of Nevada (ACAN). He was hired as an employment consultant and his duties were to help felons find work in the major hotels. Reverend Davis and Ms. Emma owed him money for the long hours he had put in, but instead of paying him they gave him excuses and eventually started to ignore him. When Cecil told the feds his side of the story and other illegal matters that definitely interested them he was instantly labeled the whistleblower. In other words, it wasn't a coincident that while under investigation, the feds discovered that a large amount of the grant funding the Davis' received to initiate a pre-release prison program was misappropriated.

On September 28, 2005, Timothy Pratt, a writer with the <u>Las Vegas Sun</u> newspaper, wrote a front page article entitled, "Baptist church leaders face federal charges." He stated that the Davis' along with Reverend McTheron Jones were arrested and charged with defrauding the government, falsifying documents, and obtaining grant funding in order to enrich themselves. They were released on bail and in spite of all of the evidence the feds had against them, the Davis' pleaded "Not Guilty."

In October 2002, Cecil Davis suspected that Reverend McTheron Jones was a phony and he took it upon himself to contact the president of C.C.S.N. They discovered that Jones' completion dates in school were incorrect and even the program his doctorate was in that was listed on the alleged diploma that always hung crooked on his wall was incorrect. Not only did he stretch the truth about his education, he also did the same about his rank in the Navy.

McTheron proudly told people that he was a Lieutenant Commander in the Navy, but he forgot when he told me the first time I met him that he was an E7, like me, which is a Chief Petty Officer. I allowed him to have his day even though I was often taken by anyone who lied about their military service. I later found out that the reason he enhanced his ranking was to feel superior to a female church member named, Annie White who was a Master Sergeant in the Air Force.

Reverend Jones taught study skill classes at Community College of Southern Nevada (CCSN). He claimed to have earned a doctorate in psychology from San Diego State University. He even went as far as to brag about his extensive educational background, and it was probably meant to justify the $75.00 a session he was charging women at Second Baptist for his "warmed over soup" counseling.

Prior to receiving the grant for a pre-release

prison program, Reverend Davis appointed Reverend Jones as an administrative assistant. His job was to write the grant and help launch the program. Cecil Davis said when the Department of Justice returned the grant with red marks requesting explanations on nearly every page. But it didn't matter to Davis; I was informed that he would receive the funding no matter what.

During a Sunday morning service, Reverend Davis looked at Cecil Davis straight in the eyes and said, "Get thee behind me Satan and leave!" The woman sitting next to me laughed and whispered, "If old Satan did that then there wouldn't be anybody left in the pulpit."

Dr. Jerry Lockhart, C.P.A., was the Chairman of the Trustees Board and I was the First Vice Chairman. Thanks to the Navy, I am a stickler when it comes to following orders; the i's must be dotted and the t's crossed.

There were nine members on the Trustees Board

and we were responsible for collecting the money during service, counting it in a secluded room, documenting the final amount in the accounting book, and placing it in a safe. At that time, the amount collected every week was between $20-$25,000. During his trial period, Reverend Davis leaned over and whispered in my ear, "Place the money collected in an envelope for the visiting pastor." I refused and that's when all hell broke loose.

He scheduled a meeting for all members to attend. The purpose was to discuss the by-laws, but it was really about who was the HNIC (Head-Nigga'-In-Charge) at the church. He was furious that I was passing out flyers and urging members to attend. He wanted the people who fell under his spell to be there, but I wanted all of the members to voice their opinion. He assumed I was undermining him so he instructed a deacon to take my flyers and make sure they were removed from the church. He told him, "And if you can't do your job then I will take my gun and go out and shoot the Nigga' now!"

The tension within the church and among the staff was too thick for my sober mind. But like I was taught in the Navy, most things don't go as planned in life and therefore you must learn how to adapt accordingly. I also learned that I "made this bed" and I was committed to making sure-like I was required in the Navy-that the covers were pulled tight, the pillow centered just under the headboard and the extra blanket was folded neatly at the foot of the rack (bed). This menial task was meant to give us sailors a great sense of pride and the motivation to do other tasks throughout the day. It's the little things in life that matter. And if you don't do the little things right, you will never do the big things right.

A member, who had no idea there was riff between them, asked Reverend Davis if he had seen Cecil. He said, "I hope he is in hell!" The member passed the insult on to Cecil but he was not moved. He said, "Here is a man who preached a sermon using geese in a singular form. At least I know the difference the between a goose and geese."

The trial of Reverend Davis and First Lady Davis began in 2005 and ended when the Davis' decided to plead guilty. On June 28, 2007, the headlines for the <u>Las Vegas Review Journal</u> newspaper read, "Minister, wife sentenced." Reverend Davis was given five years of probation, and Ms. Emma had to serve two years in prison because she was a felon. They both were ordered to pay fines and restitutions that totaled $29,500. It was the biggest church scandal in the history of Southern Nevada.

I wanted so much for the charges against the Davis' to be false, but the jury had spoken and the trial was over. This story-book ending of deceit and mistrust left a stain on the hem of the church's dress, a stain that is, to this day, still there.

A few days later after the sentencing, an emergency meeting was called at the Church and the congregation unanimously voted to have Reverend

Reverend Willie Davis was the pastor of my church, Second Baptist, for 29 years. His wife, First Lady Emma were indicted on federal charges which led to his dismissal in 2007.

Willie Davis dismissed from his position. The by-law issue he had with me was still lingering. I guess you can say it was on pause. As soon as the name of his replacement, Interim Pastor Namon Johnson, was hung on the door, he decided to take up where Davis left off. In 2001, I was voted, "Man of the Year" at Second Baptist Church. Seven years later, I was asked to turn in my keys.

One Sunday afternoon, shortly after the last service, a security guard from the church showed up on my doorstep and asked for the keys to the Trustees' office but I refused to hand them over. A few days later, a "conspiracy group", which consisted of Namon Johnson and a few deacons, scheduled a meeting in the conference room. When I walked in, I was ready for my curtain lecture.

I wasn't a bit surprised who the "chosen ones" were sitting at the table. In fact, I always suspected every last one of them. I was asked to turn in my keys and again I refused. I sat at the head of the table, dodging their bullets left and right and acting unmoved by what my consequences would be for not cooperating. I was unimpressed by their Sunday best suits, Stacey Adams shoes, and shiny gold watches. I was never afraid to beard a lion in his own den-my mama taught me that.

A week later, a special-called meeting with the members of the congregation was scheduled to decide my fate on the Board. I sat in a middle pew and glanced at the members while the Interim Pastor Namon Johnson explained the issue they were having with me. The church's vote was two-to-one in favor of my removal. I stood up and politely walked over towards a Trustee's member, but was interrupted by the security guard. He asked for the keys and I refused. I leaned over and handed them to Dr. Esther Langston, a woman who really did have a doctoral degree.

The conspirators did not hinder my pride not one bit. All I wanted to do was protect the church. I threw my chin up and went on about my business. I had things to do, people to visit, and lives to enhance-these were the only keys I needed. Damn the torpedo, full speed ahead.

- - - It is Written - - -

Nine

★
CONTENT OF YOUR CHARACTER

For the first time in my life, my health failed. In 2001, I was diagnosed with prostate cancer. After receiving 41 radiation treatments, the cancer shrunk and went into remission. Seven years later, I was prompted for out-patient surgery at a Veterans medical clinic to resolve an underactive problem with my bladder. When I woke up, I was in a flight-for-life helicopter that was headed to the Mike O'Callaghan Federal Medical Center located on Nellis Air Force Base. After a thorough evaluation, my doctor determined that I flat-lined and it was caused by an allergic reaction to one of the medications administered by the anesthesiologist.

That same year, my bladder became overactive from a damaged nerve in the muscle. I was starting to feel like people my age, but I wasn't ready to be inconvenienced by father-time so I made an appointment to correct the problem.

A normal day for me was waking up at 6:00 a.m. I would prepare a light breakfast, read a few scriptures and be out the door no later than 7:00 to either visit the shut-ins at a convalescent home, feed the homeless, check on sister and brother so-and-so, drive someone to a doctor's appointment or to the grocery store, attend a veteran's funeral, and at the end of the day participate at a church or community meeting. But since my health had declined, I was only able to carry out two and sometimes three of those missions. I did not want to lie around the house reading and watching television. Grandma Lorraine used to say that a stable can wear out a horse faster than a road.

One Sunday afternoon, I was leaving church when I noticed a flyer sitting on the mantle in the hallway. It read, "Stop the Closure of F Street." I wondered what all the fuss was about so I attended the next meeting. I learned that the City of Las Vegas forgot to inform the residents that they were going to close F Street, the community's only thoroughfare, and replace it with a brick wall, which would separate the Westside community from the billion-dollar newly developed area called "Symphony Park." I lived two blocks away and I had no idea about the closure.

When Mayor Oscar Goodman admitted he had no knowledge about the closure, the community became outraged-how dare he insult their intelligence. Even they knew a street doesn't close on its own. I laughed at the idea of trying to add another "to do" on my list, but the nudging on my shoulder was persistent and I learned long time ago to follow it. It was a good fight and I needed to get in it because I didn't want anyone at my front door asking for more than keys.

The city was bold in their move and it was important to match their strength. Every Monday, the F Street Coalition hosted meetings at the West Las Vegas Library. They gained a tremendous amount of support from the majority of the community and outside sources. Trish Geran, the Chairwoman of the Coalition, was the perfect one to organize the community. She had just finished assisting the "Obama for America" campaign headquarters, which was located at Senator Majority Leader Steven Horsford's office, with grassroots effort and familiarized the staff with the "Black" areas of town. She was the author of *Beyond the Glimmering Lights-The Pride & Perseverance of African-Americans in Las Vegas,* had experience in civil engineering, architecture, was an eloquent writer, and more importantly was raised on the Westside.

Trish said, "The country had just elected her first Black president and now we have to correct Las Vegas' Jim Crow blunder." But what really made her aggressively motivated was when she saw how hurt her mother, Hazel, was when she learned about the closure. It was the thin line nobody was permitted to cross- somebody had to pay.

Hazel lived on the Westside for over 60 years and she vividly remembered how in April of 1968, Mrs. Ethel Pearson, an 80 year old woman she regarded as her mother, single handedly demanded the City of Las Vegas to not just keep F Street open, but six other streets: A, B, C, D, E, and G.

It was a Black police officer who informed Mrs.

When the protest against the closure of F Street was in full swing, a cartoon illustration of Mayor Goodman and a representative from the city appeared in the Las Vegas Review Journal newspaper.

Pearson that the city had plans on the table that included closing streets A through G. The next day, Mrs. Pearson stormed into city hall and demanded an explanation from Mayor Oran K. Gragson. When he said he was unaware of the closures, she organized the community and held a series of meetings at Second Baptist Church. After seven days of continued protest, the city buckled. They agreed to close only five streets; F and D would remain open. Forty years later, here we are still dealing with the same problem concerning the same darn streets. Not only did they plan to close F Street they were also going to close D Street but the funding for the project was stopped just in time.

Mrs. Pearson was a member of Second Baptist and a community activist. She was a tiny petite woman who tied a knot in her stockings around her knees, roared like a lion when she smelled a whiff of discrimination, and enjoyed chewing tobacco. Spittoons were hard to find in local stores so she carried a mason jar lined with Kleenex in her purse.

Human rights activist, Ethel Pearson came to Las Vegas in 1944. For over 20 years, she single handedly fought for improved freeways, transportation, and jobs.

When Mrs. Pearson turned 100 years old, Mayor Ronald P. "Ron" Lurie (holding cake) presented her with the Key to the City. Standing is former Director of EOB Senior Center, Hazel Geran and sitting is Chairman of the EOB Board, Theron Goynes.

At times, she would schedule a meeting in her home for the politicians who represented the area. They would all attend even though they knew she did not have adequate seating. When they walked in she would say, "Son, grab a seat on the floor. That's one of the reasons God gave you a big caboose." Mrs. Pearson wouldn't dare allow the lack of anything stop her from doing what she was determined to do.

The media covered the Coalition's every move, but not even their support could stop the closure of the street. The threat of a protest and our complaints were being ignored and that's when the advisory board suggested to the community that it was time to move matters to the next level. A unanimous decision was made to file a lawsuit and attorney Matthew Callister was highly recommended.

Callister was a former Nevada Assemblyman, Senator, and City Councilman. He served two terms on the "Chairman of the Ways and Means Committee" and was a Mormon. At the next meeting, he walked in wearing jeans and a sports coat with blonde hair that fell way below his shoulders reeking of cigarette smoke. Hazel jokingly said, "There goes the neighborhood."

He said that the city should not have closed the street and agreed to take on the case for a fraction of the cost. On December 24, 2008, Christmas Eve, the Stop the F Street Closure, LLC aka F Street Coalition, filed a federal lawsuit claiming the City of Las Vegas and N.D.O.T. were in Violation of Title VI of the Civil Rights Act of 1964. The initial cost to reopen the street was estimated to be somewhere in the ballpark of $20-$70 million, but we could care less.

The newspaper blogs posted numerous hate and racist comments. The funny thing was most of the writers of these unintelligent statements had no idea what they were talking about. If you didn't know any better, a newcomer to Las Vegas would easily assume that the Westside community was "infested with criminals, and filled with a bunch of blood sucking, lazy

Assemblyman Harvey Mumford speaks to the F Street Coalition during the protest march on the Las Vegas Strip. He was there from the beginning.

I was too ill to join the protestors on the Strip, but I made sure I gave them my blessings before the bus departed from Second Baptist's parking lot.

Black people who did not want anything out of life." When in fact, there were lawyers, doctors, authors, entertainers, engineers, teachers, and casino bosses living in the area and have been for quite some time.

We continued to hold weekly meetings. The room became so packed I thought I was in another city. Our first protest marched was to city hall to state our grievances in front of city council members. They listened and were even excited we came, but our actions and words did not produce a change.

Brandon Greene, a 26 year old native Las Vegan, decided to write a letter entitled, "Silence is Deafening: Where the F(St) is Senator Horsford?" On the cover was a picture of Horsford with duck tap over his mouth and the overall message was meant to make him feel guilty for turning his back on the community where he was born and raised. The Nevada legislature was in session and Brandon made sure every representative received a copy. He ruffled a few feathers but not enough. That's when Trish-who was fully aware of the history, suggested a march down the city's Achilles heel-the Las Vegas Strip.

The Coalition wanted everyone to meet at Second Baptist Church's parking lot on Saturday, April 18, at 8:00 a.m. and from there a chartered bus would transport them a few blocks from the Strip. One of the members suggested wearing a red shirt to symbolize anger. I was recovering from bladder surgery so I was unable to march but I was there to watch the bus drive away.

The television stations broadcasted the demonstration in real-time. I was so proud. With signs in one hand, the protestors lined up like soldiers ready for combat. They were what we referred to in the military as "Battle Ready." Bonnie Greathouse, a woman with an impeccable voice, repeated the Coalition's fight song in a bullhorn, "The Westside fought the battle of F Street, F Street, F Street, the Westside fought the battle of F Street and the wall came tumbling down."

A few days later, Majority Leader Senator Steven Horsford had an idea on how to resolve the problem. He said that bill AB304 written by Assemblyman Richard "Tick" Segerblom to preserve a historical neighborhood was just sitting on a table with no place to go. The language contained the basic guidelines and standards and with a few amended areas it could be our solution.

Horsford was the youngest and the first Black senate majority leader in the State of Nevada. With his powerful position and the multiple boards he served on, the amended bill passed through the senate committee without any obstacles.

To give Horsford a little ammunition, a video recording of Estella Jimerson, a 93 year old woman who lived adjacent from the closure, was emailed to all legislative members. She looked in the camera and said, "I may be slightly blind but even I could see that the closure of F Street was wrong." She went on to say how she allowed Black soldiers to stay in her home during the war because they were not allowed to stay in White areas, and that she never would have bought her house if she knew they were going to close the street. Mrs. Jimerson was the first person to donate money to the Coalition. She reached in her bosom and pulled out a $100 bill and said to Trish, "Here, now go open that street." May she rest in peace.

One of our representatives, Assemblyman Harvey Mumford, introduced bill AB304 on the floor. His speech was so moving and convincing the vote was unanimous. Horsford worked his magic and passed it in the senate, but after Governor Jim Gibbons visited the site he said it would be a waste of money to allow this to be funded so he vetoed the bill. We were back where we started.

I gave Trish a letter to send to every representative in the Nevada legislature, including the Governor. It was handwritten, which was what President John F. Kennedy, Jr. said he preferred to receive if someone wanted a response from him.

Mrs. Estella Jimerson, celebrating her 96th birthday at her home, lived adjacent to the closure of F Street. She said that even though her eyesight was failing she could see that the closure was wrong.

As best that I could I wrote:

I served for this country for your kindred and my kindred also. The closure of this street is a betrayal of all of them and their families who served. Each of them is worth more than $70 million, which you could raise in one hour.

The bill was re-introduced in both houses. It passed in the assembly 29-13 and in the senate 19-4, which were enough votes to overturn the Governor's veto. In July 2009, AB304 was installed into law, and because the street's opening was now legally binding and a top priority, United States District Judge Lloyd George decided that the lawsuit be rendered moot and therefore an immediate dismissal was recommended.

On May 8, 2013, the ground breaking of the reopening of F Street took place. I grabbed that shovel and dug so deep my arms nearly fell off. The city hosted workshops for the residents to design panels with pictures of pioneers they wanted to represent the history of the community. They will be displayed inside the tunnel that will connect the Westside community to "Symphony Park", which is still a sour note to some in Southern Nevada. Construction cost was estimated $13 million and the completion time was 18 months. Needless to say, on December 11, 2014, the street reopened.

The F Street Advisory Board was reassured Blacks would be hired on the project, and Senator Horsford, who was elected United States Congressman (NV-4), arranged for a board he chaired called Southern Nevada Enterprise Community to oversee the project's funds and timetable. S.N.E.C. is made up of political representatives from different wards and the two members selected from the F Street Coalition are: Shondra Armstrong-the Vice-Chairwoman and myself- an Advisory Board member.

The closure of F Street received national exposure and recognition from various aspects. It was featured on the History Channel's series, "Inspector America-'Damn This City'" episode, three writers and one photographer

SNEC ADVISORY BOARD. Left-Right: Shondra Summers-Armstrong, Stop the F Street Closure; NV Senator Kelvin Atkinson; NLV Councilwoman Pamela Goynes-Brown; NV Assemblywoman Dina Neal; Clark County Commissioner Lawrence Weekly; Dr. Linda Young, NV Congressional Delegation; and, Arby L. Hambric, Stop the F Street Closure.

for Las Vegas newspapers were awarded for their outstanding coverage, and Professor Bob McGee from the University of Nevada, Las Vegas (UNLV) wrote a dissertation on the social economics of the closure and was honored in San Francisco for shedding light on the issue. He also published a book entitled, "Community Action Against Racism: The F Street Wall and The Women Who Brought It Down."

Anita Womack-Weidner, a documentary producer from New York, and her husband Fritz, who has worked for H.B.O. in the editing and duplication department for over 30 years, made several trips to Las Vegas to film key historical moments for a documentary they are producing. Their goal is to have it aired nationally on PBS. And in the spring of 2013, our youngest Advisory Board member, Brandon Greene, graduated from law school at Boston University and passed the California bar exam after his first attempt.

The community never gave up hope. There was a time when we felt disrespected by those who attended the meetings, some even tried to out maneuver us, but nothing was too serious to put back in place.

I will never forget when one of the Coalition members informed Trish that the NAACP Las Vegas Branch President Frank Hawkins, former Nevada Senator Joe Neal, and Reverend Jesse Scott from Second Baptist Church, had a meeting with Mayor Oscar Goodman to discuss F Street. They had suggested that instead of re-opening the street the construction of some sort of business would be fair. In other words, they were making a bargain on our behalf without our approval.

As usual, Mr. Hawkins was present at the next meeting as though nothing out of the ordinary had occurred. Trish informed the members about the incident and suddenly the room was silent. She looked at Frank and said, "You think I am an airhead don't you and that I don't know what I am doing. Well, let me tell you something my daddy used to tell my brothers. He said, 'Son, always remember, the dumbest woman is smarter than the smartest man.'"

I stood proud in front of the bulldozers in front of F Street like the soldier I was trained to be. This closure was the most blatant act of racism I had ever experienced in all my life.

Trish made it clear from the onset that she was simply a voice and organizer for the community and the decisions will be made by the majority not the minority. Isn't it amazing what you can accomplish when no one cares who gets the credit.

On December 11, 2014, Mayor Carolyn Gooodman and the City of Las Vegas will host a grand opening celebration for the opening of F Street. The community at large is overjoyed and couldn't be more proud of the time and effort spent to witness this day. It was well worth the five year wait.

A wall is just a wall many barked, but nothing was farther from the truth. China's "Great Wall" was built to protect their Empire against intruders and a possible invasion from militant groups. The Berlin Wall, also known as the "Steel Curtain", was a barrier to stop movement from East to West, a sure symbol of communist oppression. Brazil built walls around the Rio de Janeiro slums to keep the residents from wandering into their breath-taking hills. These walls may appear to be different, but in actuality the meaning and purpose are the same as the one that was built to separate the Historic Westside from Symphony Park.

In 2012, Harry D. Welby, a former shipmate on the USS *Palau* called to invite me to speak at the annual *Palau* reunion, which would take place in Myrtle Beach, South Carolina, but I declined due to a continuous battle with my health. I was in and out of the doctor's office, still in search of how to repair what was broken inside my body. Welby said that of the 700 men in my division, less than 100 are alive today. I think he wanted me to feel good because he knew I wasn't my old active self.

Some years ago, I spoke at this event about my life and times on the ship. It was well received and the audience was grateful to know about some of the incidents that took place during that time period and the hurdles Black stewards had to overcome.

As soon as I made a conscious decision to be still with a fork in one hand and a steak knife in the other, I received a phone call from Hope Igarashi, an activist for veterans and the Chairwoman of the Las Vegas Universal Peace Federation She said that I was nominated to receive the "War Hero" medal from her organization, founded by Dr. Reverend Moon, and I was required to attend the "Little Angels Korean Folk Ballet Honors Korean War Veterans in Las Vegas" event, which was going to be held the following day, February 11, 2012, at Caesars Palace Hotel.

The Little Angels was founded in 1962, by Dr. Reverend Sun Myung Moon and his wife Hak Ja Han. The group consist of 31 girls and one boy, and their ages range from nine to fifteen years old. It was Reverend Moon's way of expressing gratitude to the servicemen all over the world who fought for South Korea's peace and freedom during the Korean War, and for saving his life.

In 1948, Reverend Moon was arrested in North Korea for teaching lessons from the Bible and was sent to a concentration camp in Heungnam. The day before he was scheduled to be executed, Captain Alexander

Haig attacked the camps, which opened the gates and led to the rescue of the prisoners. It was said that no one had ever survived that camp after six months, but Moon served two and a half years and walked out a free man. Reverend Moon became the founder of the Unification Church, and Alexander Haig was promoted to Four-Star General by the United States Army.

The Little Angel's stop in Las Vegas marked the 22-nation Korean War 60th Anniversary World Peace Tour. It was the first American tour since 1965, when they performed in front of Five-Star General and the President of the United States, Dwight B. Eisenhower. Hope said they only entertained royalty, dignitaries, and presidents. To the people of South Korea, the Little Angels are considered beyond royalty.

There were 3,000 people in attendance at the Little Angel's ceremony. "Congratulatory Letters" from President Barack Obama, former Presidents, George W. Bush, Jr. and William H. Clinton were read to the audience. Reverend Moon (February 25th) and his wife

On February 11, 2012, the "Little Angels Korean Folk Ballet Honors Korean War Veterans" took place at Caesars Palace Hotel in Las Vegas. I was given the "War Hero" medal by the Universal Peace Federation because of my service in the Korean War.

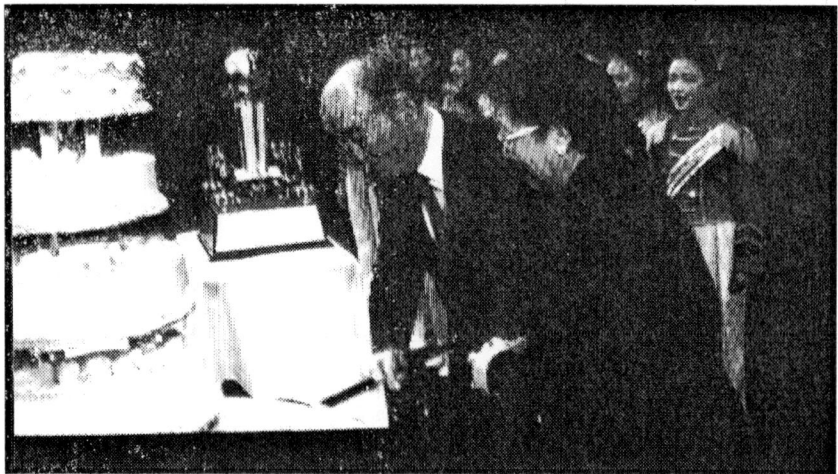

The founder of the "Little Angels" and the Universal Peace Confederation, Dr. Reverend Moon and wife Mother Ha Ja Han, celebrated their birthdays that evening.

(January 6th) celebrated their birthdays that evening. A four layered fluffy white cake with red roses swirled around the edges was carted on the stage. I got so excited. I may not be much of an eater, but sweets are definitely my weakness.

As I stood on the stage with my fellow veterans and Reverend Moon and his wife, it felt so surreal, like I was in another time period. I forgot about my health issues and concentrated on the moment. When the "War Hero" medal was placed around my neck I must have touched it at least 20 times to make sure it had not slipped off. It was medium-sized with a little weight, and boy was I ever so proud.

Approximately 20 ladies from Second Baptist Church were in the audience in spite of the fact I notified them an hour before the event started. They gathered around the stage and waved for me to come down to take pictures. I wasn't ready to say goodbye to that dreamy feeling so I slowly walked down the steps and headed towards them I shook the hands of many

Hope Igarashi (middle) the Chairwoman of the Las Vegas Universal Peace Federation recommended me for the "War Hero" medal. Hope helped to restore my hope.

F. Ronald Smith, an Owner, Operator and President of several McDonald's fast food chain restaurants served in the Vietnam War. His support meant a lot.

people, most of them I met before, but there was one in particular I had not. His name was F. Ronald Smith and he served in the Vietnam War, and was the Owner, Operator and President of several McDonald's fast food chains in Southern Nevada. I was proud and intrigued to have met such a humble and established gentleman. He looked me in the eye and shook my hand with a tight grip and said he wanted to take a picture with me. I was honored. Then I eased back on the stage. I wasn't ready to say goodnight to an event I shall never forget.

On September 3, about seven months after the "Little Angels" ceremony at Caesars Palace, Reverend Dr. Sun Myung Moon died of complications from pneumonia. He was 92 years old. He lived in Las Vegas, and one of the reasons he resided in "Sin City" was because he had a vision of transforming it into "Shining City"–a center for wholesome recreation and an international, interreligious, interracial community for world peace. The late Reverend Moon was noted as being one of the richest and most powerful religious leaders in the world.

Hope and her husband Ted, an affiliate with the Korean government, invited me to attend Reverend Moon's funeral in Gapyeong, South Korea, but the doctor would not permit me to fly on a plane.

A week later, my sister Mildred passed. She was living in Teague, Texas, and my inability to be there for her family made me feel like I did before I was drafted- incompetent and not viable. This taste of defeat churned in the pit of my stomach. I refused to become undone by fear and trembling instead I chose to will that my best years are yet to come.

I received a beautiful card from my son, Arby, Jr., and his wife Valerie. Inside was a handwritten message that said:

The Lord made us family. Miles can't keep us apart time can't make us forget trouble can't put away our hope and pride. We go on praying, we go on dreaming, we go on living with peace and courage in our heart, and we make this world a better home for all generations to come. Daddy, we try to live so that you would never be ashamed to own us as your children. We love you very much.

Valerie & Arby Hambric, Jr.

- - - It is Written - - -

Ten

★
WHO IS DRIVING THIS MULE?

On January 16, 1865, Army Union General William T. Sherman issued Special Order No. 15, which promised to redistribute 400,000 acres of land that was located along a strip of coastline in the south, in 40-acre segments to 40,000 Blacks who were under Union administration. A Baptist minister brought to General Sherman's attention that in order to cultivate the land they would need tools. Four days later, with President Lincoln's blessings, Sherman authorized the Army to loan a mule to each of the new property owners so they could be fruitful and multiply. But then the unthinkable happened. On April 15, 1865, President Abraham Lincoln was assassinated and the 400,000 acres were returned to the original owners. This crucial decision by President Andrew Johnson and his administration marked the plight of Blacks in America.

What I learned from this pivotal historical moment is this, what good is a gift if you do not have what is required to make the most of it. In this great country, one way we are guaranteed to effectively grow is if someone lends a helping hand.

One of the most life changing lessons Momma Gussie taught me was after my needs were met, what I had left over was meant to help someone meet theirs. I didn't realize what she meant until I was around 36 years old. There are few options for people struggling to make it. If no one offers to help, what are they supposed to do? I believe that one of the reasons why God blesses us is to become a blessing to others.

After I retired, in addition to my duties as a flag bearer, I made a vow to support our wounded soldiers by visiting the veteran hospital and clinics especially during particular holidays. On Christmas Day, I would place a one dollar bill inside a card for those who were bed-ridden and totally disabled and leave it on the table next to their bed. For Dr. Martin Luther King, Jr.'s birthday, the administrative staff would gather a group of patients in the recreation room to hear me recite his compelling and moving "I Have A Dream" speech.

During one of my visits, a doctor pulled me aside

and said two of his patients have begun to talk and respond and he was confident it was because of my consistent visits. Just to see a little smile on their face was always uplifting. The greatest casualty in life is to make someone feel they have been forgotten. I simply wanted them to know they were not.

In June of 2013, the Supreme Court challenged our voting rights. They claimed that the 40 year formula used in Section 5 of the 1965 Voting Rights Act needs to be updated and is unconstitutional never mind the fact that the registration and poll turn outs of minorities and seniors have proven to be immensely successful. I felt like I was living in the 40s and all of the fighting and the lives lost just to be able to vote was being ignored and disrespected. I was so angry I wrote a letter to First Lady Michelle Obama. It read:

Dear First Lady Michelle Obama,

I, Arby L. Hambric, USN Ret., recently learned that the U.S. Supreme Court has dishonored all members of the armed forces and their families who reside in the suppressed areas by voting down on the most important sections of the Voting Act. Slavery, Jim Crow, and racism are no different today than when I was growing up in the deep south of Texas. Racism and segregation was thick yet acceptable regardless that there were no laws to support this crude act of mannerism. It was a direct attack against the United States Constitution, the American Flag, and the Declaration of Independence. Could this be the "outsiders" long awaited plan to wipe us off the face of the earth? Is this the reason they have been beating us over the head with a big gun and a thick stick for the past 300 plus years?

Of the four to five decisions made by the Supreme Court, may God be the glory and may God come forth with a better plan. It's never too late to fight for freedom. No one should have the power to hold in a cage our right to vote. Slavery is over please let "them" know!

With My Highest Regards,

Arby L. Hambric
P.O. First Class, USN Ret.

Colonel Gerald D. Curry, who retired from the Air Force after serving 27 honorable years, made an outstanding response to this life altering decision. He said, "On June 25, 2013, we witnessed the Supreme

Court walk hand-in-hand with the Klan and those with a conservative agenda by limiting our access to vote." Jim Crow may have left the building, but he left behind a grandson and granddaughter who happen to be a hell-of-a politician.

On July 31, 1942, a Black man named Milton Sayles paid a $3.00 poll tax to vote in Las Vegas, Nevada. He was so proud to have been able to walk up to that booth and mark which politicians he wanted to represent his district that he kept the original receipt. He told his family that it was priceless and later in life they would understand what he meant.

The early 1940s marked the first boom on the Strip. The city offered a "wild west" experience mixed with glamour and entertainment. Thousands of tourists flocked to see the "Eighth Wonder of the World", Hoover Dam, and because most of these visitors were White, the City of Las Vegas found it necessary to racially segregate public facilities, the hotels and casinos, and designate an area of town for us Blacks to

Milton Sayles moved from Oklahoma to Las Vegas in 1940 to work at the newly completed Hoover Dam project. He was a Mason and very active in his lodge.

In 1942, Milton paid a $3.00 poll tax to vote in Las Vegas, Nevada. His family will forever cherish this receipt.

live on called, The Westside. This "understood" Jim Crow rule also applied to famed entertainers and servicemen of all ranks in the military.

Milton was born in Depew, Oklahoma in 1909, and relocated to Las Vegas from Phoenix, Arizona, because his Masonic Lodge brothers said there were more jobs than people. He found work, sent for his family, and made Las Vegas his new home. As a young man, he worked on the railroad, which was considered one of the most dangerous jobs. They called him "Pigmeat" because if he made one wrong move he would end up slaughtered like a pig. Only tough guys worked on the railroad.

His son Mitchell was a Corporal in the Marine Corp, fought in the Vietnam War, and is an active member in the Southern Nevada Chapter Buffalo Soldiers 9th & 10th Horse Calvary Association.

After the Civil War in 1866, through an act of U.S. Congress, legislation was adopted to create six all Black Army units. These fighting men represented the first

Left-Keith White, John John Everett, and Mitchell Sayles at the November 11, 2014, Veterans Parade. They are members of the Southern Nevada Chapter Buffalo Soldiers 9th & 10th Horse Calvary Association.

Black professional soldiers in a peacetime army. They were part of the building of America. It was the Cheyenne Warriors who gave them their name. They saw two things in the men that were similar to the Buffalo: a ferocious fighting spirit and naturally curly hair. On the great plains, they were the primary line of defense and they never lost a scrimmage or a battle. The Buffalo Soldiers will forever be considered legends of the west.

Mitchell can recall the story that was passed down to him about the poll tax receipt. Well, that time has come and he definitely understands the reason his daddy described what he thought as "just a piece of paper" as priceless. It was unconstitutional for the City of Las Vegas to ask Milton Sayles to pay to vote, but at least he got the chance even though some speculated if our ballots were cast.

On November 2, 1920, in Ocoee, Florida, July Perry and Moses Norman made a courageous attempt to vote. When they arrived at the polls, they were turned away but refused to leave. Their boldness and persistence caused the town Whites to get so nervous and paranoid they viciously attacked every Black folk they could find in hopes to wipe out the entire population.

As I look back, the common thread sewn within every decade of my life was yanked from the cloth of injustice. In order for future generations to continue the fight, the moment a situation arises, they must win the victory. The tide of history is a powerful weapon and the right to vote is our most powerful nonviolent act. He who controls the vote controls the land.

I am often asked why I wear my "War Hero" medal every day, which was given to me by the Universal Peace Confederation. First and foremost, while I was stationed oversees the Korean people treated us better than our own when we returned from the war. Secondly, it serves as a reminder of how far removed I am from the cotton fields of Texas. Lastly, it is a door opener. People recognize I am a veteran and sometimes they make a special effort to thank me. I vibe off their generosity; it gives me hope. I know that I speak for all of my shipmates when I say that we could never get enough thank yous for our service in our lifetime.

On Sunday, November 9, 2014, Second Baptist Church's Hospitality Ministry recognized me as the "Veteran of the Year." I was given a card congratulating me. Inside it read, "Behind every success is effort, behind every effort is passion, behind every passion is someone with the courage to try."

Epilogue

In my early years, when I was heavily engrossed in being a Navy officer more than a Black man, I was often asked my reason for putting my life on the line for a country and military that treated me like a second-class citizen. They had a point, but it wasn't valid.

I can remember like it was yesterday when a White officer said to me, "Hey my steward houseboy can you fetch me my hat." Instead of allowing someone's bitterness steal my sweetness I decided to change my attitude. Besides, I learned long time ago that the only person I wanted to get even with was someone who has helped me in some aspect. I thought of my role as a manservant for top leaders in the Navy as someone who was loyal and could be trusted, a man who was respected and highly effective. These humble thoughts have made a soft cushion for me to sit on today. Promotions are nice and medals are special but I figured I came here with nothing and I will leave here with nothing.

After President Truman dismissed Five-Star General Douglas MacArthur from his duties during the Korean War, he gave a "farewell speech" in front of the U.S. Congress. His uniform was bare-not a ribbon or medal in sight. Here stood a man who earned, after 52 years of service, over 100 hundred medals from the United States and other countries wearing a uniform with no reminders. It was an obvious message to politicians and to the military that he was hurt and that his service was all for nothing. His speech was interrupted by fifty ovations, and in the end, he borrowed a ballad from an old song, "Old soldiers never die they just fade away."

We are all engaged in some kind of battle and our will to survive makes us all soldiers. To win, you must have honor, commitment, and courage and learn when to sacrifice when it is necessary. The players may have changed but the game is still the same. In fact, the only thing that has changed is technology, and the only thing that will never change is the word of God.

I believe that if we focus less on our differences and more on our common attributes this world would be a better place. War is hell, but the cost of not protecting freedom is far, far greater. I could only pray that Blacks in the military helped to create a change for the better in society. I lived with an all-colored unit and worked with an all White staff, and I can honestly say that I have no preference. When I served in those three war eras (WWII, Korean, Vietnam) I wanted prejudices to be buried in the snowstorm of World War II, the racial slurs from Viet Cong be forgotten, and the graves of all soldiers be restored.

Yes I served under the direction of five presidents, traveled across the Atlantic and Pacific oceans, visited 10 countries, lived on the east and west coasts, was stationed on six ships, and have presented the American flag to more than 1,000 families at veteran funerals, but what I know for sure is that my life was never about me-it is about the service I provide to

In May 2013, I spoke at the West Las Vegas Arts Center's "Community Awareness" event. The crowd was receptive when they learned about my journey–a journey I wouldn't change.

others.

It was the grace of God and my family commitment that kept me focused. The military taught me discipline, respect for others with emphasis on authority. It was a tool I was given to see the world, to see my life in comparison of others, and to see the laws of man versus God in action.

I may have a low count in both ears from years of loading ammunition on ships, a shaky hand writing, a diminished appetite, and less years ahead than behind me, but thank God Almighty to *Thee* I still can *See*.

- - - It is Finished - - -

BOOKS/BIBLIOGRAPHIES

Allen, Robert L. *Story of the Largest Mass Mutiny Trial in U.S. Naval History*, Warner Books, Inc., 1989.

Blackmon, Douglas A. *Slavery by Another Name: The Re-Enslavement of Black Americans from the Civil War to World War II*, Doubleday, 2008.

Daly, James A. & Bergman, Lee. *Black Prisoner of War: A Conscientious Objector's Vietnam Memoir*. University of Kansas, 2000.

Denton, Jr., Admiral Jeremiah A. & Brandt, Edwin H. *When Hell Was In Session: Admiral Jeremiah A. Denton*, WorldNetDaily, 1998.

Erenberg, Lewis A. *The Greatest Fight of Our Generation: Louis v. Schmeling*. Oxford University Press, 2005.

Fletcher, Marvin. *America's First Black General: Benjamin O. Davis, Sr., 1880-1970*. University of Kansas Press, 1989.

Forbes, Camille F. *Introducing Bert Williams: Burnt Cork, Broadway, and the Story of America's First Black Star*. Basic Civitas, 2008.

Geran, Trish. *Beyond the Glimmering Lights—The Pride & Perseverance of African Americans in Las Vegas*. Stephens Press, 2007.

Govenar, Alan. *Lightnin' Hopkins: His Life and Blues*. Chicago Review Press, 2010.

Grimes, Herman L., Jr. *Quest for Recognition of A Father's Invention: A Son's Journey to Uphold His Father's Legacy.* Milligan Books, Inc., 2008.

Hirsch, James S. *Two Souls Indivisible: The Friendship That Saved Two POWs in Vietnam.* Houghton Mifflin Company, 2004.

Historical Foundation-The Navy, Rizzzoli International Publications, Inc., 2012.

Myers, Barton A. *Executing Daniel Bright: Race, Loyalty, and Guerrilla Violence in a Coastal Carolina Community, 1861-1865,* Louisiana State University Press, 2009.

Myler, Patrick. *Fight of the Century: Joe Louis Vs. Max Schmeling,* Arcade Publishing, 2012.

Paige, Leroy Satchel & Lebovitz, Hal. *Pitchin' Man: Satchel Paige's Own Story.* Mecklermedia Corporation, 1992.

Rhoden, William C. *Thirty Million Dollar Slave: The Rise, Fall, and Redemption of the Black Athlete.* Random House, 2006.

Tischauser, Leslie, V. *Jim Crow Laws,* ABC-CLIO, Incorporated/Landmarks of the American Mosaic, 2012.

Washington, Booker T. *Up From Slavery,* The Heritage Press, 1970.

Watkins, Mel. *Stepin Fetchit: The Life and Times of Lincoln Perry.* Pantheon Books, 2005.

MAGAZINES

Curry, Gerald. "The Future of Your Vote." *Las Vegas Edition - The Urban Voice*, 19, 1 (July, 2013).

"Jet Magazine." (19 January, 1956.)

NEWSPAPERS

Day, Jim. Cartoon illustration that said, "F Street Closed. I Think that street needs a better name… How about Jim Crow Avenue…!?" *Las Vegas Review Journal*, 6B, 1 (19 May, 2009).

Jones, Maudra. "The Life of Ethel Reece Pearson–Pioneer, Leader, Activist." *Las Vegas Sentinel Voice* 5, 2 (30 Sept. 1982).

Knight, Jennifer. "CCSN Teacher Accused of Fraud." *LasVegas Sun*, 1, 1 (7 Oct., 2002).

McLellan, Dennis. "Bernard S Jefferson, 91; Respected Appellate Judge and Legal Scholar." *Los Angeles Times*, (2002, March).

Nast, Thomas. Editorial cartoon criticizing the usage of literacy tests for African Americans as a qualification to vote. *Harper's Weekly*, v. 23, p. 52. (1879, Jan. 18).

Newspaper Account of a Meeting between Black Religious Leaders and Union Military Authorities, clippings from *New York Daily Tribune*. (1865, February 13).

Pierres, Les. "Complaints Seeks to Nix Street Closure", *Las Vegas Sentinel Voice*. (2008, December 25).

Pratt, Timothy. "Baptist church leaders face federal fraud charges." *Las Vegas Sun*, (2005, September, 28).

Taylor, F, Andrew. "Pastor was pivotal to Baptist church." (2007, June, 27).

United States Attorney's Office: District of Nevada. "Local Church Leaders Plead Guilty to Unlawfully Obtaining and Misusing Federal Grant Funds." (2007, February, 20).

Vecsey, George. "A Final Ring For Joe Louis." *New York Times.* (1981, April 17).

"Minister, wife sentenced." Las Vegas Review Journal. (2007, June 28).

INTERVIEWS
Bell, Ester with Trish Geran, 2 June 2013
Bell, J.D., with Arby Hambric, 5 June 2013
Bland, Sterling, with Trish Geran, 26 May 2014
Buford, Eugene "Peve" with Trish Geran, 10 July 2013
Busby, Ernest with Trish Geran, 25, 28, 30 August 2013
Collins, Eugene with Trish Geran, 25 June 2013
Davis, Cecil with Trish Geran, 10, 22, August 2013
Finley, Buford with author, 8 April 2013
Geran, Hazel with Trish Geran, 12 July 2013
Givens, Alfred with Trish Geran, 8 August 2013
Haynes, Rosa Lee with Trish Geran, 25, 28, 30 August 2013
Hill, Howard with Trish Geran, 18, 24 June 2013
Isom, John W. with Trish Geran, 28 May 2014
Rhodes, Deborah with Trish Geran, 20, 22 August 2013
Robinson, Pearl with Trish Geran, 24, 27 January 2014
Webb, Ranzo with Trish Geran, 15, January 2014

PICTURES COURTESY OF
Brain Jones (Scientist & Photographer Jonesblog)

Brian Berger (Sam Lightnin' Hopkins/Categories: HiLo Heroes) Courtesy of AP Press
Gardner Family
Geran Family
Gerd Matthes, Germany (Capt. Cleaves Dinner in Tacoma, WA)
Hambric Family
Hill Family
Mayfield Family
National Naval Aviation Museum
National Naval Aviation Museum (Cleaves & Fitzpatrick)
Naval War College Found. (Major Cherry & Lt. Halyburton)
NavSource Online: Escort Carrier Photo Archive
Ows.edb.utexas.edu (Colored/White Fountain)
Rhodes Family
Robinson Family (James & Pearl)
SI/CNN Photo Gallery (Satchel Paige)
Tony Mair – Photographer (Arby Hambric – F Street)
U.S. Naval Historical Center Truman on USS U-2513
White Family (Floyd, Jr.)
www.seaforces.org (Truman Leahy)
www.tuskeegee.edu (Daniel "Chappie" James)

NAVY DOCUMENTS REFERENCED
Arby L. Hambric's signed/sealed DD214
Mustering Out Payment summary
Certification of Vessels & Stations

WEBSITE CREDITS
David Farragut, First rear admiral, vice admiral, and admiral in the U.S. Navy. Paraphrased: "Damn the torpedoes, full speed ahead!" wikipedia.org/wiki/David_Farragut.
flickr.com/photos/vieilles_announces

Joe Louis the Brown Bomber, 1991 April 12.

Penny Liberty Bow Files, Wordpress, February 15, 2012.

The Navy Department Library, *The Negro In The Navy. Guide to Command of Negro Naval Personnel.* NAVPERS-15092, NAVY Department Bureau of Naval Personnel U.S.G.A.

U.S. Administrative Naval History of World War II #84.

(United States Gold Association) *Paving the Rhodes for other African-American Golfers,* by Rhonda Glenn.

Index

Adams, George, 218

Air Force, United States, 76, 133, 138, 139, 172, 179, 181, 191, 194, 195, 199, 219, 229, 264

Air Tran Ron VR-8, 119

Ali, Muhammad, 227

All-American High School Bowl, 190

Alliance Collegiums Association of NV, 217

Amos 'n' Andie (tv show), 38, 284

Arlington National Cemetery, 199, 202

Armour & Company, 40

Armstrong, Shondra, 246, 246

Army, United States, 35, 66, 67, 75, 165, 172, 199, 202, 253, 261, 267

Assembly Bill 304, 241, 242, 244

Atkinson, Kelvin, 246

Bainbridge, Maryland, 45

Barrow, Joe Louis "Brown Bomber", 197

Battle Ready (song), 240

Berbick, Trevor, 197

Beverly Hills, California, 133, 200,

Beyond the Glimmering Lights: The Pride & Perseverance of African in Las Vegas, 232

Birmingham, Alabama, 91

Black Eyed Pea Festival, 15

Black Prisoner of War: A Conscientious, Objector's Vietnam Memoir (book), 127

Boligee, Alabama, 214

Booker T. Washington High School, 24, 41

Boston University, 247

Boulder City, Nevada, 215, 216

Brashear, Carl, 86, 88, 90

Brer Rabbit Blackstrap Molasses, 137

Brooklyn Dodgers, 203

Buckley, Argyll E., 99

Buckley, William F., Jr., 99

Buffalo Soldiers, 48, 267, 269

Buford, Eugene "Peve", 172

Busby, Ernest, 138, 139, 141, 181, 186

Busby, Mildred, 18, 137, 185, 186, 259

Bush, George W. Jr., 253

Cadillac, 215

Caesars Palace:
   Hotel & Casino, 203, 252, 257
   Pavilion, 198

California Lottery, 216

Callister, Matthew, 236

Camp Ellis Company 'B', 165, 284

Captain's Mess, 61, 63, 73, 96, 102

Carson, Johnny, 208

Centerville, Texas, 12, 172

Charlottesville, Virginia, 199

Cheetah (dog), 116, 159, 160

Cherry, Fred V., 124-126

Chesapeake Bay, 55

Cheyenne Warriors, 269

China, 95, 96

Christmas Bombings, 123

Civil Rights Act of 1964, 91

Civil Rights Act Title VI, 237

Civil Rights Movement, 284

Clark Air Force Base, 124

Cleaves, Willis E., 52, 58, 60, 61, 65

Cleveland Indians, 138

Clinton, William "Bill", 76, 253

Cole, Henry, 29, 103

Cole, Mary, 31

College of Southern Nevada, 218, 219

Compton, California, 134, 135

COMTRA PAC, 116

Connor, Theophilus Eugene "Bull", 89, 91, 92

Corsicana, Texas, 137

Crockett, Texas, 158

Crow, Jim, 17, 19, 34, 48, 92, 168, 232, 264, 265, 267

Cruiser Division 16, 107, 112-114

CrusdesFlot-1, 115

Cumberland Golf Course, 208

Curry, Gerald D., 264

Dallas, Texas, 14, 42, 45

Daly, James "Jim" A., 124, 127, 128

Dauhl, Captain, 65

Davidson, John, 111, 117

Davidson, North Carolina, 125

Davis, Benjamin O., Jr., 66, 69, 70

Davis, Benjamin O., Sr., 65, 69, 199,

Davis, Cecil, 179, 180, 217-220, 222

Davis, Emma, 201, 202, 205, 206, 212, 213

Davis, Jeanette, 212, 213, 215

Davis, Willie, 170, 171, 177, 180, 212-220, 222-225

Declaration of Independence, 264

Denton, Jeremiah A., 104, 105, 121-124

Denver, Colorado, 183

Department, United States Justice, 220

Depew, Oklahoma, 267

Desflot-1 (Flotilla), 106

Detroit, Michigan, 202, 213

Dodge Ramcharger, 175

Douglas, Frederick, 14

Dunlap, Captain, 103, 104

Economic Opportunity Board (E.O.B.), 235

Eisenhower, Dwight D., 253

Elder, Lee, 208, 210

Elizabeth River, 55

Ernie's Bar, 164, 165

Everett, John John, 268

Evers, Medgar, 199

Executive Order 9981, 75, 141

FASRON 108-VP7, 92, 95, 97

Federal Bureau of Investigations, 216, 217

Fitzpatrick, W.C., 52, 60

Flying 10, 49

Fort Riley, Kansas, 203

Fort Worth, Texas, 40, 42

G.I. Bill, 133

Gapyeong, Korea (South), 258

Gardner, Dyshell, 187-189, 191

George, Lloyd, 244

Geran, Hazel, 232, 235, 237

Geran, Trish, 231, 232, 236, 239, 242, 248, 250

Germany, 38

Gibbons, Jim, 242, 244

Good Conduct Certificate, 120

Gooding, Cuba, Jr., 88

Goodman, Carolyn, 250

Goodman, Oscar, 231, 234, 248

Goynes-Brown, Pamela, 246

Goynes, Theron, 235

Grade of the Commander of the Order of the Star of Africa, 67

Gragson, Oran P., 234

Gravely, Samuel L., Jr., 76

Great Wall, 250

Greathouse, Bonnie, 240

Greene, Brandon, 239, 247

Grimes, Herman L., Jr., 58

Grimes, Herman L., Sr., 57, 58

Gunther, Madison, 207

Haig, Alexander, 253

Halifax, Nova Scotia, 63

Hall, Georgia, 159, 164

Hall, O.C., 31, 159, 164

Halyburton, Porter A., 125 , 126

Hambric, Arby L.:
Birthplace-13, Enlisted in Navy-45, Second Class Petty Officer-64, sails to Liberia-65, Admiral's staff-106, Wife dies-141, moved to Las Vegas-164, joins Second Baptist Church-169, visits family-189, "War Hero" medal-253, appointed on SNEC board-246

Hambric, Arby, Jr., 147, 189, 258

Hambric, Dorothy, 190

Hambric, Joe, 16

Hambric,, Sam, Sr., 15, 17, 18, 21, 157, 147, 182, 183

Hambric, Valerie, 258, 259

Hanoi, Vietnam, 123, 124, 127

Harper, Vicki, 187, 189

Harrison, Alma, 93-95, 99-102, 147

Hawkins, Frank, 248

Haynes, Rosa Lee, 17, 186

Heungnam, North Korea, 252

High Desert State Prison, 192

Hill, Bunnie, 134

Hill, Howard, 132, 134

Hirohito, Emperor of Japan, 46

Hiroshima, Japan, 46

Holmes, Larry, 197

Historic Westside, 167, 168, 230, 232, 237, 240, 245, 251, 267

History Channel, Inspector America, 245

Hollinsworth, Lt. Commander, 97

Home Box Office (HBO), 247

Hoover Dam, 265

Hopkins, Abe, 157, 158

Hopkins, Sam "Lightnin", 157, 158, 160

Hopwood, H.G., 113, 114

Horsford, Steven, 231, 239, 241, 242, 245

Houston, Texas, 14, 156

Hughes, Howard, 197

I Have A Dream (speech), 263

Igarashi, Hope, 251, 256, 259

Igarashi, Ted, 259

Illinois, Chicago, 165, 205, 208

Indian Springs, Nevada, 192

Internal Revenue Service (IRS), 202, 204

Ives, Burl, 145

Iwakuni Air Force Base, 95, 97, 135

Iwakuni, Japan, 95

Jackson Street, 169

Jackson, Jesse, 198, 212

Jacobs, Willie, 212

James River, 56

James, Daniel "Chappie", 76-78, 199, 281

Janeiro, Rio de, Brazil, 250

Japanese Navy, 58

Jefferson, Bernard S., 200

Jefferson, Joseph, 171

Jehovah Witness, 127

Jimerson, Estella, 241, 243

Joe Louis 'The Champ' Golf Course, 208

Johnny Walker (scotch), 94, 103, 137

Johnson, Andrew, 261

Johnson, Floyd, 157

Johnson, Johnny, 170, 172

Johnson, Namon, 225, 226

Jones, McTheron, 228, 219, 220

Kaye, Danny, 108, 145

Kennedy, John F. , 91, 199, 242

King Neptune, 71

King, Martin Luther, Jr., 262

Kings James Version (Bible), 169, 192

Kirby, George, 165, 167

Klu Klux Klan, 91, 265

Knox, Frank, 53

Korea, Republic of (North), 86, 89, 252

Korea, Republic of (South), 89, 252, 253, 258

Korean Police Action, 97

Laboa (Chief Steward), 61, 62, 73, 63

Lachocotte, Commander, 116

Langford, Mary, 157

Langston, Ester, 226

Lankford, Artice, 18-21

Lankford, Mildred, 18, 137, 185, 258

Las Vegas Metro. Police Dept., 174, 178

Las Vegas Review Journal, 223

Las Vegas, Nevada, 159, 164, 167, 168, 178, 181, 194, 199, 212, 212, 215-218, 230, 231-237, 240, 247, 248, 250, 252, 253, 257, 265-269

Leahy, William D., 98

Leaping 16, 49

Leona, Texas, 157

Levels, Charlie, 22, 35, 39, 42, 50, 137, 156, 183, 184, 195, 208, 210

Lincoln, Abraham, 261

Little Angels Korean Folk Ballet, 252, 253, 257

Littlejohn, Courtney, 190, 202

Lockhart, Jerry, 220

Long Beach Naval Shipyard, 107, 208

Long Beach, California, 105, 117

Los Angeles, California, 107, 111, 113, 153, 173, 203

Louis, Joe "Brown Bomber (see Barrow), 38, 197-200, 202, 204, 208

Louis, Martha Jefferson, 197-200, 202, 203

Lurie, Ronald P. "Ron", 235

Lynch, Willie, 56

MacArthur, Douglas, 96, 98, 273

Marine Corp, 267

Marquez, Texas, 13

Marshall, Thurgood, 82

Masters (golf tournament), 210

Mayfield, B.T., 170-172

McAdams, A. B., 137

McAdams, Gussie, 15, 39, 149, 182, 183, 185, 186, 195, 262

McAdams, Henry, 16

McAdams, John, 15, 36

McAdams, Loraine, 13, 15, 34, 36, 182, 230, 237

McDonald's, 257

McKee, Robert "Bob", 247

Melbourne, Australia, 108

Men of Honor (film), 88

Mercedes Benz, 214

Mexia, Texas, 181

Midland, Texas, 22

Mike O-Callaghan Fed. Med. Center, 229

Miracle on Madison, 198

Mizzell, Dekeara, 187, 190
Mizzell, Taquan "Smoke", 187, 188, 190
Moffett Federal Airfield, 118, 119
Monrovia, Liberia, 73, 74
Moon, Ha Ja Han, 252, 254
Moon, Sun Myung, 252-255, 257, 258
Moore, Willie, 53
Morgan, Rose, 200, 201
Morse Code, 123
Mt. Zion Church, 147
Mumford, Harvey, 238, 242
Myrtle Beach, South Carolina, 251
N.A.A.C.P. Legal Defense Fund, 82
NAACP Las Vegas Branch, 248
Nagasaki, Japan, 46
Nashville Hall of Fame, 208
Nashville, Tennessee, 111, 208
Naval Air Station Moffett Field, 118, 119
Naval Air Station Quonset Point, 92, 93
Naval Reserve Training Center, 51, 52
Navy Diving & Salvage School, 88
Navy, United States, 45...
Neal, Dina, 246
Neal, Joe, 248
Negro Calvary, 48
Negro Troops, 67
Nevada Dept. of Transportation, 237
Nevada Test Site, 164
Nellis Air Force:
  Base, 206, 241
  Commissary, 181,
  White Hall, 193, 195, 206
Nettles, Mary, 170, 172
New Bethlehem Baptist Church, 146

Nixon, Richard M., 76
Norfolk Harbor, 101
Norfolk Naval Base, 54, 188
Norfolk, Virginia, 54, 55, 58, 75, 86, 93, 101, 125, 148, 189
Norman, Moses, 269
O'Connor Hospital, 152
Obama for America, 231
Obama, Barack, 253
Obama, Michelle, 263
Oceans:
  Atlantic, 54, 274
  Pacific, 95, 105, 112, 116, 133, 274
Ocoee, Florida, 269
Officers Candidate School, 203
Old Soldiers Never Die (song), 273
Operation Homecoming, 123
Pacific Palisades, California, 133
Pacific Reserve Fleet, 105, 284
Paige, Leroy Robert "Satchel", 138-140, 142
Panama Canal, 54
Parke-Davis, 146
Patterson, Floyd, 202
Patterson, Mother Letha, 191
Pearson, Ethel, 232-236
Peck, Gregory, 145
Perry, July, 269
Philadelphia Experiment, 101
Philadelphia Naval Yard, 101
Phoenix, Arizona, 135, 177, 182, 267
Pinkstonia, Veronica Clara "Ronnie", 111, 112, 115-119, 131, 132, 134, 135, 136, 144, 145-148, 149, 150, 151-155, 159, 161
Plan of the Day (announcement), 86

Polywog, 71

Port Chicago Disaster, 80-82

Pratt, Timothy, 218

Prisoner of War (POW), 123, 124, 128

Professional Golf Association (PGA), 207, 208

Project Rainbow, 101

Public Broadcasting Station (*PBS*), 247

Pudget Naval Sound Base, 54

Purple Heart Medal, 58

Quonset Point, Rhode Island, 92

Reagan, Ronald, 199

Red Skelton Show (tv Show), 38

Red Tails, 67

Redd Foxx Show (tv Show), 38

Redwood City, California, 147

Reid, Leonard, 206

Reno, Nevada, 172

Rhodes, Claudia, 205

Rhodes, Deborah, 205, 209

Rhodes, Peggy, 205

Rhodes, Theodore "Ted", 205, 206, 208, 210

Rice, Thomas Dartmouth "Daddy", 33

Rio de Janeiro, Brazil, 250

Roberts, Joseph Jenkins, 55

Robinson, Edward G., 145

Robinson, Jackie, 203

Robinson, James, 176

Robinson, Sugar Ray, 203

Rolls-Royce, 214

Royal Oldsmobile, 162

San Bruno, California, 118

San Diego Naval Shipyard, 115

San Diego Open (golf tournament), 208

San Diego State University, 219

San Diego, California, 111, 175

San Francisco, California, 80, 118, 247

San Jose, California, 118, 132, 150, 152, 156

Santa Clara, California, 118

Sayles, Milton, 265, 266

Sayles, Mitchell, 267-269

Schmeling, Max, 38, 199, 203

Scott, Jesse, 248

Scott, Jewell, 215

Sears Roebuck & Company, 26, 132, 144

Second Baptist Church:
  Brotherhood, 173, 174, 177
  Deacon Board, 176
  History, 171, 176
  Male Chorus, 179, 180, 217
  Mother Board, 172
  Trustees Board, 220, 225
  Usher Board, 176, 177

Segerblom, Richard "Tick", 241

Shell-Back, 71

Sherman, William T., 261

Shields, Eddie, 178

Shining City, 257

Sin City, 257

Shippen, Hanno Smith, 209

Shippen, John, 208

Sifford, Charlie, 210

Sinatra, Frank, Jr., 212

Skates, Robert, 205

Smith, F. Ronald, 256, 257

Sodom & Gomorrah, 212

Southern NV Chapter Buffalo Soldiers 9th & 10th Horse Calvary, 267

Southern NV Enterprise Community, 245

Special Order 15, 261

Spiller, Billy, Jr., 208

Spiller, Billy, Sr., 207

Squadron, 99th Pursuit, 76

St. James Methodist Church, 147

Stacey Adams, 226

Starks, Leonard, 153, 156

Starks, Ruby, 153-156

Steel Curtain, 250

Stevensville, Texas, 142

Stop the Closure of F Street (*F St. Coalition*), 230-238, 241- 247

Street Car Molly, 55

Symphony Park, 230, 245, 251

Tarleton State University, 142

Teague, Texas, 19-21, 24, 33, 39, 41, 42, 102, 135, 141, 149, 156, 182, 183, 187, 258

Ted Rhodes Golf Course, 208

Tijuana, Mexico, 112, 115

Tonieville, Kentucky, 87

Tree of Life, 14

Triplett, Matthew, 146

Truman, Harry S., 75, 82, 86, 88, 89, 96, 141

Tubman, William V.S., 66, 74

Tuscaloosa, Alabama, 214

Tuskegee Airman, 69, 76, 79

Unification Church, 253

United Methodist Church, 28, 31

United States Colored Golf Association, 205

United States Congress, 267

United States Constitution, 83, 264

United States Golfers Association, 207

United States Military, 41, 123, 215

United States Naval Training Center, 45

United States Supreme Court, 71, 263-265

Universal Peace Confederation, 252, 254, 256, 264

University of Nevada, Las Vegas, 247

University of Virginia, 188

USS Navy Ships:
    Aldrige, 101
    Helena CA-75, 115
    Los Angeles CA-135, 107-109, 112
    Palau CVE-122, 50, 54, 57, 60, 65-68, 74, 79, 86-89, 91, 92, 251
    Piedmont AD-17, 115, 116
    Sarsfield, 98

Vacation Bible School, 29

Veterans Admin. Regional Office, 141

Viet Cong, 121, 123, 125, 128, 274

Vietnamese, North, 121

Vietnamese, South, 119

Virginia Beach, Virginia, 188

Voting Rights Act of 1965, 263

VP 7 Squadron, 95

Waco, Texas, 26, 138

Warren, Willis, 177

War Hero (medal), 252

Wars:
    Civil, 48, 267
    Korean, 78, 88, 95, 95, 133, 134, 252, 273
    Pearl Harbor, 58
    Vietnam, 78, 107, 113, 118, 119, 121, 123, 124, 127-129, 173, 257, 267
    World War I, 54
    World War II, 46, 58, 76, 173, 202, 205

Washington, Tacoma, 51, 54

Watts, Lacey, 185

Watts, Minnie, 31

Waxahachie, Texas, 15

Webb, Ranzo, 174-177

Weekly, Lawrence, 246

Weidner, Anita-Womack, 247

Weidner, Fritz, 247

Welby, Harry D., 251

Wells Fargo, 175

West Las Vegas Arts Center, 275

West Las Vegas Library, 231

WESTPAC (western pacific), 112, 113, 115

When Hell Was in Session (book), 124

White, Annie, 219

White, Floyd "Buckshot", 191-195

White, Keith, 268

Wilburn, Erwin "Brother", 165, 166

Wilkerson, Bobby, 141

Williams, Jerome, 190

Woods, Tiger, 210

XVI Olympics, 108

Young, Linda, 246